The Power of Self-Coaching

The Five Essential Steps to Creating the Life You Want

Joseph Luciani, Ph.D.

WILEY

John Wiley & Sons, Inc.

Published by John Wiley & Sons, Inc., Hoboken, New Jersey
Published simultaneously in Canada

Design and composition by Navta Associates, Inc.

For general information about our other products and services, please contact our Customer Care Department within the United States at (800) 762-2974, outside the United States at (317) 572-3993 or fax (317) 572-4002.

Wiley also publishes its books in a variety of electronic formats. Some content that appears in print may not be available in electronic books. For more information about Wiley products, visit our web site at www.wiley.com.

Library of Congress Cataloging-in-Publication Data
Luciani, Joseph J.
    The power of self-coaching : the five essential steps to creating the life you want / Joseph Luciani.
        p. cm.
    Includes bibliographical references and index.
    ISBN: 978-0-471-46360-3
1. Self-actualization (Psychology) I. Title.
    BF637.S4L83 2004
    158.1—dc22   2004005661

10 9 8 7 6 5

Contents

iii

Contents

Acknowledgments

I'd like to thank my wife, Karen, my son, Justin, and my daughter, Lauren, for their continuous love, encouragement, and unselfish sacrifice these past few years. Without them my journey would be without meaning.

The healing power of Self-Coaching was never something I devised or fabricated. It was revealed to me through my patients, all of whom courageously allowed me to join them in their unique struggles. They have been my teachers. Together we've learned to recognize one of life's essential truths: that we must take responsibility for life—not by compulsively trying to control it, but by separating fact from fiction and yielding to a deeper, more spontaneous life-force within.

Had it not been for my agent, Jean Naggar, and her exceptional staff, the dream of expanding the power and promise of Self-Coaching would never have been realized. From the start, Jean has been a source of inspiration and unflagging encouragement. Her extraordinary literary talent and intuition are the sole reason my program has been making its way around the world today.

My editor at Wiley, Tom Miller, who from the beginning was able to see the value of my work, has once again proven his artistry. I marvel at his remarkable ability to look at a manuscript and extract its deeper, underlying essence. His insights have made all the difference. I am eternally grateful to Tom for his loyalty, enthusiasm, vision, and friendship.

My literary journey began many years ago, and I've been blessed to have Jane Rafal accompanying me every step of the way. Jane has advised, coached, encouraged, and convinced me to believe in myself as an author. Her editorial contributions and support have contributed immensely to the growth of Self-Coaching as well as to my personal development as a writer.

Finally, I'd like to thank my friends and family members for their support and helpful suggestions: my lifelong friend and brother-in-law, Ron "Coach" York; my cousins, Celeste Galdierei (the family CEO) and Cathy Mangano; my nieces, Chrissy Lamm and Kathy Maki; my dear friend and mentor Perinkulam Ramanathan; my longtime confidant and buddy, Dr. Alan Gettis; my friend and lawyer, Alex Locatelli; and a special thanks to three wonderful ladies who taught me well, my mother, Mary, my Aunt Tessie, and my mother-in-law, Joan.

Preface

My father wasn't a happy man. The stress of his constant anger is probably what killed him at age fifty-two. As did his lack of exercise, lack of self-discipline, deplorable diet, and aversion to doctors. Toward the end of his life he was drawn to gambling—it represented a way out of his cul-de-sac existence. Hitting it big and winning the trifecta represented hope in what was otherwise a sea of hopelessness.

I look back at my father now and my heart aches. His life and early death were such wastes. If only I could have shared with him what I know now. If only I could have helped him recognize that there were choices. Like so many people, my father considered himself a victim of fate. It would never have occurred to him that his ineffective, frustrated life was nothing more than the result of cultivated habits of negativity. If only I could have told him about the power of Self-Coaching.

In more than twenty-five years of private practice I've come to realize that my father's tormented life wasn't that unusual. Many people wind up in therapy complaining of nagging, vague problems such as feeling overwhelmed, worrying about the future, or having general feelings of unhappiness, helplessness, or self-doubt. Some find their way into therapy because there's nowhere else to turn; everything in their lives has begun to crumble. Most people, I suspect, never make it into therapy. They just live with their problems, not realizing they have a choice.

Do you have your own laundry list of unresolved problems? If these diffuse, rather low-grade complaints are allowed to fester, they can lead to more serious emotional problems. But why wait for depression to develop or for anxiety to slam you into a panic? Why not recognize that the friction you feel in your life is a clue that you've drifted away from your natural and spontaneous center, your capacity for genuine happiness. Self-Coaching can bring you back to where your life begins to make sense, where you begin to flow effortlessly with life rather than desperately trying to control it.

Learning to live more naturally and spontaneously may seem complicated, especially if you're suffering. It's not complicated at all. It isn't your nature to be unhappy or to suffer, it's simply your habit! And the truth is that habits are learned and habits can be broken. All habits. No matter how destructive, a habit can't hurt you if you learn to stop feeding it. How do you feed a habit? Every time you worry, fret, fear, or doubt, you're throwing your habit crumbs of your insecurity—feeding it. *The Power of Self-Coaching* will introduce you to a powerful tool called Self-Talk, which will starve the habits that hurt you and let you choose the life that serves you.

So get ready to take your life back from the grip of reflexive, habituated thinking. Once you do, you'll understand my attitude toward more complex, traditional methods of healing. And if I sound a bit cocky, that's okay. Because Self-Coaching isn't about reflection or philosophical meditation, it's about instilling a can-do fire that will enable you to have the life you want, the life you deserve.

In my previous book, *Self-Coaching: How to Heal Anxiety and Depression,* Self-Coaching was presented with the specific goal of alleviating the symptoms of anxiety and depression. Over the years since I first introduced Self-Coaching, I've found that my method is applicable to a much wider range of problems than just anxiety and depression. You will find *The Power of Self-Coaching* to be an empowering guide that can eliminate emotional friction in your life and reconnect you with an innate capacity for genuine happiness—before more serious emotional problems develop. Long after you've eliminated insecurity and struggle from your life, Self-Coaching can continue to serve you as an ongoing source of strength and rejuvenation.

The power of Self-Coaching relies on the fact that you can learn to defeat whatever holds you back in life. Whether it is panic, depression, social anxiety, laziness, ineffectiveness, lack of success, or unhappiness, you must defeat whatever holds you back from the life you're capable of having. And you can! By following the five essential steps outlined in this book, you will find the uncomplicated answer to all your self-generated problems. You will learn to move from control thinking to a more spontaneous, instinctual understanding of what you need to be happy.

Introduction

Choose to Change, Choose the Life You Want

Destiny is not a matter of chance, it is a matter of choice;
It is not a thing to be waited for, it is a thing to be achieved.
—William Jennings Bryan

I find no better place to begin this book than by introducing you to Tracy, a single, forty-eight-year-old retail clerk who came to see me to ask one question—a question I've heard many times before. Perhaps it's a question you've asked yourself:

> All my life I've struggled. I've worked hard for thirty years and have nothing to show for it. No husband, no kids, no career, nothing. I live my life in this filthy, one-room apartment over-looking a parking lot and the roof of a Chinese restaurant. On a good day I drink too much wine, I watch too much TV, and I eat too much junk. On a bad day I don't get out of bed. I worry about dying, I worry about living, but mostly I worry about being alone for the rest of my life.
>
> Sometimes I can't sleep, my mind races, thinking about opportunities I've missed and people I've hurt. I get headaches and stomachaches, I'm angry at everyone and find it impossible to

trust. My doctor wants me to consider depression medication, but, to tell you the truth, I'm not sure I want to bother. So what if medication makes me feel better? I still live in this apartment, still don't have a decent job or a family. Why bother?

My doctor also tells me my blood pressure is too high, I'm overweight, and unless I change my ways, I'm headed for a heart attack. Change my habits—what a joke. I *am* my habits! Sure, Doc, I'll just go home and change! Doesn't he get it? This is me, stuck, destructive, and destined to live out my days alone and miserable. And I'm so scared.

I came to therapy to ask you one question and I'd like an honest answer: *Can someone like me really change?*

How would you answer Tracy's question? Many seem to think the personality is fixed at birth: "He's been a control freak all his life. I don't expect him to change." Or, "Sure I'm anxious. My mother was anxious, and so was her mother. It runs in the family." Some seem unsure: "Ever since my surgery I've gone downhill. I wasn't always such a worrier. I just can't seem to get back to feeling secure again." And yet for others, it's not a matter of personality, it's a matter of fate: "Some people are blessed with good fortune. Me, I've had nothing but bad luck all my life." The questions remain: Do people change? Can an unhappy life be exchanged for one of happiness and success?

What Do You Think?

I pondered these questions for years, from both intellectual and personal standpoints. Struggling with insecurity and anxiety as far back as I can remember, I wanted to know the truth. And yet, as much as I wanted to change, there was always a part of me that felt I was chasing rainbows. *People don't change, not really.* Even when I gave myself the benefit of doubt, the question remained: *If change is possible, can it be enough to make a significant difference in my life?*

Is Therapy the Answer?

I find that most people who come for therapy usually arrive with a guarded ambivalence about whether it's possible to change. For some, after years of struggle and frustration, therapy is often their last hope to learn life's secret formula for happiness. And who is the keeper of this secret? The psychologist, of course.

There's no doubt about it: a psychologist can inherit a lot of projected power. The psychologist becomes the healer, the teacher, the guru—and all before a single word is ever exchanged! Because of these projections, most people go through an initial infatuation period where just being in the psychologist's presence sends them off feeling "the best I've felt in years" and touting the amazing benefits of therapy. Then, as the sessions progress, things begin to slow down. Symptoms, initially eclipsed by the euphoric belief that finally you're getting the help you need, begin to return, along with the distressing realization that nothing has changed. Or worse, the fear that nothing *will* change! This can be a real letdown as the infatuated energy gets replaced by the mundane work of historical exploration, week after week after week. It's during this postinfatuation period that many begin to feel disillusioned, recognizing there's no abracadabra magic involved in change.

As therapy progresses, most people reluctantly give up hope for an epiphany or secret insight, one that's supposed to set them free. Instead of waiting for that startling breakthrough or quick fix, they're left with the tedious work of figuring out *why* they do what they do. And by this time they're months into therapy and still acting like the same old wretch. What can they do? They've already invested all this time and money . . . maybe a few more sessions? A few more months?

What's the verdict? When it comes to therapy, what's the consensus? Is it just a palliative shoulder to lean on and nothing more, or is it a tool for legitimate personality change? The question needs to be asked: Does therapy work, does it hold the secret of change? The short answer is *yes* and *no*. But before making sense of this paradox, I first need to tell you what I learned from my own years of struggle and from my training analysis.

Yes, Change *Is* Possible

I took my personal analysis very seriously. After all, if I was going to dispense sage psychological advice, I couldn't feign being healthy—I had to become healthy. This I did manage to accomplish. I'm not bragging, I'm just letting you know from the outset that *yes*, change is, in fact, possible. I actually became a different person, with different perceptions, different thoughts, and different behavior. "Different" may not be the correct word because I was still me, I didn't wake up one day feeling I was someone else. But my experience of life certainly was different. I no longer felt congested and bottled up with my habits of overthinking and worry. I began to relax and enjoy a spontaneity that had always eluded me. I was actually living my life for the first time rather than *thinking about* living my life. And these experiences have made all the difference.

If you asked me what changed me, I couldn't tell you. Not at first. But after many years of analysis and struggle, I somehow managed to change. I became a better person, no longer driven by insecurity and reflexive defense. The problem was that I couldn't put my finger on *what* changed me. Being a psychologist and being curious, I had to find out. Was it my Jungian or Freudian analysis? My Gestalt or trans-actional group analysis? I couldn't tell you because my change came *after* I had finished all these experiences, not during. Perhaps it was the cumulative effect of all of the years and all of the insights and effort. Whatever it was, I needed to know. And I needed to be able to explain it to others.

As it turned out, my hunch was correct: it wasn't any one thing that turned my life around, but a combination of all my psychological efforts. Being a consummate opportunist, I took bits and pieces from each of my therapeutic experiences and, over time, combined these insights with all I had learned in more than twenty-five years of listening to people. And that brings us to Self-Coaching. I've been able to condense into five simple steps what took me a lifetime of struggle and curiosity to figure out—five essential steps to creating the life you want. Funny thing, the solution to the riddle of how we change isn't that complex or difficult. But like any riddle, until you know the punch line, it can drive you crazy.

Say Good-bye to the Medical Model

What exactly is the mechanism that promotes change? Notice I didn't say "promotes healing." That's because I think it's time we moved away from the medical model that has dominated psychology for the past hundred years. What's the medical model? Well, for starters, if you go to therapy, you're considered a "patient." If you suffer from anxiety, depression, or any other recognizable "symptom," you have a mental "illness." And to describe what's tripping you up in life, you look to the "doctor" for a "diagnosis." This is a physician-based medical mentality.

Okay, I'll try to be fair. Psychology grew out of the psychiatric influence of the early masters—Freud, Jung, Adler—all of whom were physicians, influenced by the medical model of healing. It's only natural that their ideas were influenced by their medical training. Unfortunately, this bias became rooted in the culture of therapy and to this day still winds up affecting how we think about psychological problems. In the classic 1948 film *The Snake Pit*, Olivia de Havilland portrayed a woman institutionalized in a crowded state hospital due to a breakdown following depression. The snake pit of the title is the hospital's room of horrors, an open ward in which the hopeless cases are confined. This groundbreaking film, along with many others that followed, has contributed to our perception and fears of mental illness.

When I was nine years old, I overheard my father telling my mother that if he didn't learn to relax, he was going to have a nervous breakdown. (When I grew up, in the fifties, "nervous breakdown" was a generic term used to describe anyone who had to be hospitalized for psychological reasons.) *Nervous breakdown!* I was petrified. What was this terrible thing that was wrong with my father? For a while I was afraid to ask, but my fear eventually forced me to approach him and ask for details. Unsuspecting that I had overheard his conversation, my father casually explained that if you ever had the misfortune of having a nervous breakdown, "men in white coats come to your house and take you away in a straitjacket." If this wasn't enough to set my thoughts spinning, he continued, "They put you in a padded room and give you medication and sometimes electric shock." *Electric shock!* That was it—my head was swimming. Not noticing my apparent distress, my father concluded, "When you have a nervous breakdown, you lose your mind."

That's all I had to hear: *You can lose your mind!* I was distraught. I can't say for certain, but I think it was that same afternoon that I went to the library and took out my first book on psychology, Freud's *The Ego and the Id.* I couldn't understand a single word of it, but just having it in my possession made me feel safer. I should point out that by the ripe old age of nine, I had already become a consummate worrier. I used to worry about everything: my parents dying, schoolwork, who liked me and who didn't. So don't think I was going to let this nervous breakdown thing die. After all, what if nervous breakdowns were inherited? That very afternoon I decided no nervous breakdown for me. I wasn't about to lose my mind! No, sir, not if I could help it.

Such was my introduction to psychology.

As I see it, the term "nervous breakdown" has become almost extinct, only to be replaced by the more ambiguous term "mental illness." What is your reflexive association to the word "illness"? When you're ill, you need to see your *doctor,* right? Why is this? Because an illness is something that happens to you, you don't necessarily cause it, you're powerless to do anything about it, and therefore you can't be responsible for curing yourself. This definition takes the concept of "healing" out of your hands and puts it in your doctor's—where it should be with a physical illness.

As far as I'm concerned, it doesn't matter if you go to a neighborhood clinic or travel to Vienna for your therapy, healing . . . wait, let me stop myself here. From now on, rather than using the term "healing," I will use the more appropriate term "change." That said, regardless of whom you seek for treatment, no therapist in the world can change you. Change—all and any change—has to come from you. This is worth repeating: the capacity for creating the life you want resides within you. A therapist can facilitate that change, but so can you, with some insight and direction. That's where Self-Coaching comes in. But first, a bit of background.

"Yes, Dear"

I had just gotten my doctorate and was involved in acquiring the necessary training analysis to apply to the Jungian Institute. My analysis had been going on for a few years (that's right, years) when one day I was complaining about not having enough free time, not having enough money, and not having enough fun. Now, I don't know if it was intentional or whether it was a calculated response or whether it was just his frustration, but my analyst interrupted me with the overly sarcastic comment "Yes, dear . . ." I didn't hear a word he said after that. I was mortified, shocked, embarrassed. How dare he insult me like that? I left his office in a huff.

Those words hung in my consciousness and refused to let go, *Yes, dear.* In that moment, what was pointed out was the lunacy of my ongoing, forty-dollar-an-hour whining! "Yes, dear" was telling me—or that's how I interpreted it—that not only wasn't I being mature about my problems, but also I had gone over to the other side, I was acting like a child, and a wimpy one at that. Those words just kept echoing in my mind like a bell. The nerve! How dare he?

It wasn't until after I had discontinued my therapy that the bigger truth was able to reach me: he was 100 percent right—I was acting exactly like a whining, whimpering child. I had unconsciously assigned the lofty designation of "parent/protector/keeper of life's secret" to my analyst, and I was expecting him to take care of me and make it all better. My job was just to show up each week and free-associate (which for me was a euphemism for complaining) about the problems du jour. When he said those now-pivotal words, something in me shifted. It was—well, not at first, but in the weeks, months, and years that followed—an insight that allowed my life to turn on its axis. Those two seemingly magical words—"Yes, dear"—need to be explained so you can understand the core motivational starting point of Self-Coaching.

Don't Be Addicted to Rescue

I don't think I'm that different from most people who enter therapy. In each of my therapeutic experiences (I've had a few), I entered therapy expecting to find answers. And in each case I fully expected my therapist to have those answers. It never occurred to me that he didn't. Or, for that matter, that I was at all responsible for this understanding. Week after week I would offer up my trials and tribulations, waiting for profound insights, one of which—I was sure—would change my life.

Week after week I left feeling mildly disappointed, unburdened—a bit lighter, but no different. In part, I wasn't getting better because of my expectations. When you enter therapy you naturally begin to hand over responsibility for your problems to the therapist. You quickly get used to sharing what, until now, were totally your problems and burdens. And with this sharing, you feel a sense of relief. I see this all the time. Someone will report after a first session, "Doctor, I feel so much better. I haven't felt this good in a long time." This phenomenon reflects the infatuated experience I mentioned above, and it's also part of the relief you experience from what I call "unburdening."

Unburdening can be appropriate in times of stress or duress, but as a style of life it becomes regressive and childlike, especially when you begin to believe that *I don't have to deal with this now, I'll just wait until I see my therapist.* Once you become convinced that you don't have to handle your struggle anymore, or worse, that you can't handle it, and Dr. So-and-so can, then the die is cast. Why do you think people remain in therapy for years and years? It's because they've become convinced they can't possibly do any of this psychological problem-solving on their own. As self-trust dwindles, you become susceptible to addiction—an addiction to being rescued.

In this way, a therapist can easily become a crutch. When you sprain an ankle, a crutch is indispensable. But as the sprain heals, it becomes imperative that you discard the crutch and strengthen the leg. If you neglect to exercise and strengthen your ankle, what happens? The muscles atrophy and you lose function in your foot. At this point you declare, "I can't walk without my crutch." The same thing can happen in therapy. If, after a period of time, your ego begins to lean too heavily on the therapist, your ability to handle life atrophies. You become convinced that you can't possibly function without your therapist's advice.

This is why when I meet with someone who is anxious or overly controlling, one of the first things I tell him or her is that my approach is not traditional, that in the interest of developing maturity and personal responsibility, I don't want them to call me between sessions with hysterical outbursts or questions. (I do, however, first establish a foundation of why and what we're trying to accomplish and give full instructions for any emergency situation; that is, any situation in which there is doubt about maintaining personal safety or ensuring the safety of others.) At first, most will struggle with this limitation because it seems counterintuitive: therapists are supposed to rescue you! I once worked with a man who, shocked by my policy, asked: "You mean you want me to handle my own problems?" Yup, I did!

Jean, a twenty-eight-year-old secretary, came to me after a long history of anxiety-related problems. It was evident to me after our first session that Jean wasn't going to be a happy camper. Jean had long ago abandoned any capacity for self-trust and had since been to a string of psychologists and psychiatrists, looking for someone to take on her burden. Her calls became so childlike, so self-defeating that I saved one of her voice messages to play back for her:

> Dr. Luciani, I know you're not going to call me back, but could you please reconsider. I really need to talk to you. I really do. Honest! Someone at work said I was obsessing about something and I don't know if I made a fool out of myself. I'm driving myself crazy worrying and I need you to call me back as soon as possible. I don't want to wait until our next session. Please call me right away. I know you're there! Just this one time, I promise I won't call again. Please, please, please call me. I don't want to struggle like this. . . . I need you to call . . . right now!

Jean was giving in to a childish reflex that insisted that whatever she needed to handle life, *she* didn't possess it. She was convinced that I possessed the magic words to stop her pain. And you know what? There was a grain of truth to her fantasy. Had I returned her call, she would have felt cared for, she would have felt that someone handled the situation and that her world wasn't going to end. She would have hung up the receiver feeling fine. This had been a typical scenario for Jean with her former therapists until they got fed up with her constant barrage of phone calls. One therapist told her, "Don't you know you're bothering me? Can't you just leave me alone for one weekend?"

Jean was addicted to being rescued. I, from the start, had a much bigger objective in mind. We had to break her reflexive habit of leaning on others and instead begin to establish self-reliance and trust. The only way this could begin was to get Jean to tolerate her fears and hysterics. After I gave her a foundational understanding of her need for control, I had to give her a few pep talks. I had to convince her that her habit of insecurity wanted her to believe she couldn't handle the challenges of her life—but the truth was, she could. She needed to develop some muscle—ego muscle. The first step was to help her understand that it was imperative for her to struggle through her weeks without using me as a life preserver.

She hated it and me for a while, but slowly the calls diminished. Jean would often plod into our sessions huffing and puffing: "Yes, I got through this week. Yes, on my own, thank you!" But soon she began to realize the single most critical point I was trying to make. She recognized that since I wasn't going to bail her out, she had to do something to feel better. The operative word here was that *she* had to do something. This was the beginning of the end of Jean's suffering.

Shortly after this insight she informed me, "Since I knew you weren't going to call me back, I decided to handle the situation on my own." Although full of resentment, she did it. She actually did it! And believe me, I was very enthusiastic about pointing this out to her (along with a bit of a pep talk): "You're really doing a great job. Don't feel you need to understand everything right now—just getting through these panicky times and not quitting on yourself, that's the first step. Fantastic! Great job!"

Jean and I are finishing up her treatment as I write. It has been a few months, and during this time I can report that not only do I never get any hysterical phone calls, but also Jean has learned that what she was looking for from me was something that truly existed within her. It was there all along. She just didn't know it. She's no longer psychologically frail; now she has real ego muscle.

What about you? Do you believe, or can you believe, that you can find everything you need by looking within? If you're like so many others, you may have become conditioned to burying your head in the sand. If this is the case, you're probably caught up in a life of compensation, seeking meaning and answers externally (money, power, status, or control), or you've become plagued with symptoms of emptiness, anxiety, or despair. Take a close look at your life. See it as a mirror would. And just as a mirror reflects the reality of your physical image, so your life experiences can reflect an accurate image of your personal evolution if you learn to interpret what you see.

Let's start with quality of life. Are you generally happy? Content? Successful? Or do you feel unhappy, downtrodden, and defeated by life? Specifically, what are your symptoms? Do you get bored with things and people? Are you experiencing depression, tension, stress? These are all part of insecurity's reflection. Self-Coaching is going to use this information to change your life. And don't start whining about being confused or overwhelmed, because if you do, I have two words for you: "Yes, dear."

The Dynamics of Change

As previously stated, all change begins with an acknowledgment that the power to transform your life comes from you. Self-Coaching is going to teach you that accepting this responsibility means challenging the shabby thinking that has compromised your life.

The misguided person who rejects personal responsibility is convinced that there is an easier way: *if only I could hit the jackpot; if only she would say yes; if only I could get that promotion.* "If only" is a statement of despair and an avoidance of responsibility. What you're really saying is "If only such-and-such would happen, then I'd take responsibility." It's as bad as the "Yes, buts": "Yes, I want to change, but it's too hard." What about you? Are you excusing yourself from taking responsibility? Are you talking yourself into a life of stagnation?

You can begin the process of change right now, by looking for limiting terms such as "if only" and "yes, but." Begin to develop some psychological muscle by realizing the truth about what's going on in your life rather than excusing yourself from it. Becoming more conscious of life's responsibilities will serve as a springboard for the Self-Coaching that's ahead.

Pick the Life You Want

It may seem incomprehensible that you can actually pick and choose the life you want. But Self-Coaching can convince you by:

- teaching you *what* to change
- training you *how* to change
- convincing you that you can do it

When I first started driving I knew nothing about my Volkswagen's internal combustion engine. On those few occasions where something did go awry and I found myself stuck on the side of the road, I'd wind up popping the hood and randomly poking around, hoping that magically I'd touch something that would revive my recalcitrant Beetle.

After one particularly frustrating experience, I was determined to do something about my helplessness. I purchased a repair manual from the dealer and decided to make friends with my engine. It wasn't long before I was changing spark plugs, setting valve clearances, and adjusting the timing. Not too shabby for a beginner. As time went on, my confidence and expertise grew. The ultimate test came while my wife and I were traveling cross country. We had just entered South Dakota's Badlands National Park and pulled off the road to view the desolate beauty of the landscape. Getting back into the car and turning the key, I was greeted not with the familiar sounds of ignition but with a disconcerting silence! Had it been a few months earlier, I would have been left to my aimless poking, but now I knew I had legitimate options.

Getting a screwdriver from my tool kit, I confidently slid under the car, located the starter solenoid, and placed the blade of my screwdriver across its two protruding screws. With a crackle and a spark, the engine fired right up. The solenoid had gone bad and needed to be jump-started. Rather than spending a night in the Badlands, we were off for points east—me, with a smile that lasted for many miles.

When it comes to cars, trial-and-error, hit-or-miss mechanics is rarely successful. The same goes for psychological problems. If something breaks down in your life and you blindly begin poking around, chances are you're not going to stumble on the answer. The first step in change is to lay a foundation of understanding and consciousness. You need to know what the problem is if you're going to fix it. Instead of an auto-repair manual, you have a Self-Coaching one. In the chapters that follow you're going to be introduced to the simple truth about psychological struggle. And trust me, it's not as complex as an internal combustion engine. In fact, I'm going to boil it all down to two words: "control" and "habit." You'll see.

Getting back to my car metaphor, once you understand what the problem is—let's say it's a leak in the master cylinder—you don't need to know *why* it began leaking (history), you only need to know how to fix it. The *why* isn't important; the *how* is. The five steps of Self-Coaching will give you all the tools you need for any repair. Whether it's an emergency or just routine maintenance, you'll know how.

The final step in change is motivation. You need to be convinced you can do it. What to change and how to change are worthless without the energy that sustains these efforts. Remember Jean, earlier in this introduction? Her ego was so enfeebled, she had gotten used to demanding that her therapists take care of her every panic. As a result, the panics became more frequent instead of less. The plain and simple truth is that without the ability to believe in yourself and to translate that belief into ongoing effort and desire, you will go on struggling.

If self-doubt, distrust, and insecurity have managed to estrange you from life's true source of happiness, Self-Coaching can teach you to reclaim it. It really can! Just ask yourself one question: "What's stopping me?" Answer: "Nothing!" There's nothing in your way. Never was!

The question remains: Why are some people prevented from experiencing success while others are seemingly blessed with it? Is life nothing more than a lottery ticket where you either have the right numbers or you don't? This fatalistic notion didn't sit well with me. It's not fate that dictates success or failure, happiness or unhappiness, but what we do with our fate. As Shakespeare put it, "The fault, dear Brutus, is not in our stars, but in ourselves."

If the fault is in ourselves, what can we do to steer our fate toward happiness and personal empowerment? This was the question that prompted me to expand my original technique of Self-Coaching, which I had been successfully using in therapy for years specifically to treat anxiety and depression. What you hold in your hands is a much broader, more evolved program capable of teaching you that change—all change—is not only possible, it's not even that difficult. Not with a foundation of understanding, a systematic training program, and the power inherent in a Self-Coaching approach.

PART I

The Promise of Self-Coaching

1

Self-Coaching: Get the Power

Barbara, a fifty-two-year-old insurance salesperson, had been struggling with apathy for years in her marriage, in her lackluster career, and in her life. Like those of many people, Barbara's problems weren't serious or debilitating enough for her to seek therapy. After all, she had always managed to get by—one way or another. She was a woman who had long ago conceded to a life of self-deprecation, doubt, and hesitation. Why? No reason—well, at least no rational, here-and-now reason. It had simply become her habit. It was only because of her frustrated husband's instigation that Barbara—with her typical ho-hum, detached attitude—agreed to talk with me. After a few months of Self-Coaching using the techniques outlined in my previous book, *Self-Coaching: How to Heal Anxiety and Depression,* Barbara had an epiphany:

> Funny how you come to accept a view of yourself—even if that view is distorted! For most of my adult life it's as if I've been building a case against myself. Looking for reasons to say "I'm not okay!" Perhaps the biggest lesson I've learned these past few months is that I have a choice. For years I've been choosing—without really thinking about it—to accept a decrepit view of myself! Can it really be true that now I can simply choose to "not choose" negativity? The truth—once you see it—seems so simple,

so obvious, yet for most of my adult life it's been eluding me. Then again, I haven't been looking that hard.

I'm not exactly sure what triggered my complete turnaround, but it happened, and I'm feeling intoxicated! It's as if everything became clear all at once. My life is changing before my eyes, almost as though all I've had to do is set the course and turn the switch. How can it be so easy? How could I have missed seeing it all these years?

Now that I'm finally beginning to see myself clearly, I need to ask: What's my first step toward satisfaction? I need to determine what I want or need. I realize that what I want or need may not exactly be what Tom wants or needs, so we must continue to talk and somehow mesh our goals. I hope our compromise will give both of us a sense of satisfaction. The very act of trying to work it out is a positive move, but really only one step in the right direction. Tom is thrilled that I'm not the way I was, that I am trying. Thinking about how I was (thoughtless, impetuous, anxious, depressed) is sobering. For now I'll be on my guard against careless actions, lazy patterns, thoughtless remarks and responses. But I must say, with my new attitude, nothing seems impossible any longer.

Stripes to Spots

You've heard it said that humans are creatures of habit. If you're anything like Barbara, you've probably never given this notion much thought, especially if you've been trying to figure out why your life seems to be wasting away, forever stuck in second gear or, worse, in reverse. Whereas other people seem so much more successful and downright blessed, you keep plodding along wondering when—or if—your time will ever come. Perhaps you have a dead-end job or a seemingly unending string of bad luck, or one personal rejection after another. Many people I've worked with come to me suspecting an assortment of reasons for their unhappy lives, but rarely—if ever—do they suspect the culprit to be nothing more than bad habits. Convinced instead that fate has been conspiring against them, many feel victimized by life, looking to be rescued from their own powerlessness and despair.

In twenty-five years of private practice you learn many things about human nature. You'd probably be surprised if I told you that many people who come into therapy aren't actually looking to change. It's true. What they really want is to become better neurotics! The perfectionist, for example, wants to become more perfect without feeling that nagging, uncomfortable anxiety all the time. The worrywart simply wants a lifetime guarantee to eliminate all those nasty surprises. And the compulsive workaholic isn't looking to slow down, just to get a good night's sleep once in a while.

How many times have you said, "I really have to change," only to go on and on with your incessant rituals? A big part of why you struggle is because you've become attached to your problems—your insecurity is the tar and your bad habits the feathers. And as uncomfortable and difficult as these habits may be, you're so identified with them that you'll actually argue with anyone who suggests that you try to change them. "But, Doctor, you don't understand, I've been a nervous wreck all my life. How do you expect me to relax?" Or, "There are people who live charmed lives and then there are people like me. Everything I touch turns sour. It's just the way it is."

If you're like most people, you probably feel that leopards can't change their spots. For leopards this may be true, but for you it's dead wrong. If you've been limited by your "spots," whatever they may be—lethargy, anxiety, self-doubt, fear, panic, depression, apathy, or even bad luck—then you need to be convinced that the power for change, real change, is a choice that Self-Coaching can teach you to make.

Self-Coaching Reflection
An ineffective, unhappy life is learned.

The fact that they weren't born ineffective, unhappy, frustrated, or insecure seems to elude many people. Regardless of what you may think, a life of struggle consists of learned patterns of perception and reacting. And if all your problems are, in fact, learned, then the good news is that whatever trips you up can be unlearned. In the chapters that follow you'll learn that the quest for control is the motor behind your unhappiness. But more important, you'll learn one of life's best-kept secrets: controlling life is a myth! Life simply cannot be controlled.

For now I have only one question for you: why do you go on struggling with your life if you're unhappy? Maybe it never occurred to you that you don't have to struggle, especially if you've become identified with your problems. You might, for example, throw up your hands and admit, "Yes, I'm lazy, it's my nature." In this case you're admitting that there's no difference between you and your laziness. Another reason may be that you've become a slave to the faulty perception that more control is the answer to your problems. "I can't let anyone see me without my makeup. What will they think?" Whatever the reason for your struggling, stumbling life, why not change? You can, and Self-Coaching can teach you how—not by trying to control your problems, but by living without them.

Before going farther, let's start off with a simple self-quiz to determine the quality of your life. After learning to incorporate the power of Self-Coaching into your life, you may want to retake this quiz to prove just how much you've changed. Then again, you may not want to bother—since you'll already know how much happier your life has become. You'll have the power.

Quality of Life Self-Quiz

Please read the following questions carefully, but don't overthink your responses. Circle your responses as being either mostly true or mostly false as they generally pertain to your life. Answer each question even if you're not completely sure. Scoring is at the end of the test.

T   F   I'm not a very positive person.

T   F   I usually wake up with a sense of dread about beginning my day.

T	F	I seem to have many regrets.
T	F	I'm often jealous of other people.
T	F	I hate my job.
T	F	I'm not as happy as other people.
T	F	I have many fears.
T	F	I'm often moody and/or depressed.
T	F	I worry/ruminate a lot.
T	F	I seem to have bad luck.
T	F	I often have thoughts that begin with "If only . . ."
T	F	I'm insecure.
T	F	I'm often too negative.
T	F	I've had one or more panic attacks in the past six months.
T	F	I usually don't feel that I'm as good as other people.
T	F	Life is a constant struggle.
T	F	Something always goes wrong.
T	F	I have many self-doubts.
T	F	I'm a great procrastinator.
T	F	I'd much rather be safe than sorry.
T	F	I waste too much time.
T	F	I often find myself "what-iffing."
T	F	I'm often anxious or tense.
T	F	In relationships I often feel competitive.
T	F	I suffer from unexplained physical difficulties.
T	F	I often have nightmares.
T	F	I've been treated for anxiety or depression.
T	F	I always expect the worst.
T	F	I don't have many interests or hobbies.
T	F	I get bored too easily.

T	F	I spend too much.
T	F	I'm not a good listener.
T	F	I have no willpower.
T	F	I'm lazy.
T	F	I'm always tired.
T	F	I have a hard time saying no to others.
T	F	I watch too much TV.
T	F	I don't sleep well.
T	F	I fear getting older.
T	F	I often hold grudges.
T	F	My looks are too important to me.
T	F	I have trouble falling asleep.
T	F	I'm stingy.
T	F	I often drink too much.
T	F	I don't adjust well to changes.
T	F	I can't stay focused at work.
T	F	I'm not very efficient.
T	F	I always find fault in others.
T	F	I'm always feeling rushed; there's never enough time.
T	F	I don't consider myself an emotionally strong person.

Total your "true" responses. A score of 14 or fewer suggests that you have a satisfactory quality of life. Self-Coaching can teach you to cultivate an even deeper awareness, spontaneity, and enjoyment of life.

A score of 15 to 30 suggests that the quality of your life is significantly restricted. For you, it's safe to assume that Self-Coaching will make a significant difference in your overall happiness.

A score of 31 or more suggests that the quality of your life is substantially compromised. Self-Coaching can make a profound difference in the quality of your life.

Choosing Power

It's time to stop making yourself miserable and start learning how to jump-start your life. You hold in your hands a powerful and unique program that works. For years I've been incorporating my Self-Coaching technique in my practice as well as assisting readers from all over the world. The results confirm, over and over again, that success and personal happiness—on the job, in relationships, or in your own mind—is a choice you can learn to make. Sounds kind of simple, huh? With the right understanding and uncomplicated coaching program to implement it, it is.

Self-Coaching is going to connect you with your inner power to no longer feel victimized by circumstances, self-doubts, or even bad luck. You can choose to create the life you want by training yourself to be a complete and successful person. And make no mistake, the power that can transform your life isn't something you have to develop or create—all you need do is unleash it! It's always been a part of you, hidden by insecurity, waiting for you to turn it loose.

How do you turn your power loose? Simple: remove the obstacles of self-doubt and insecurity that are blocking it. If you do this, your power will find you. It's up to you. If you already possess the power, why not use it? The only thing you have to lose is your misery.

Self-Coaching Reflection
**Who you are, what you are, and where your life is going
are all choices.**

This notion that you have the power to choose the life you want may take some getting used to. I'd like to take the concept of choice a step further. As I see it, life itself is choice. The person you are at this moment is really the end result of all the life choices you've made to date, even though that may be difficult to believe. Just as a building is made of many individual bricks, each life choice you've made has contributed to the person you are today—choice by choice. The sooner you learn to take responsibility for the choices you make, the thoughts you have, and the attitudes you embrace, the sooner you can have the life you want.

Self-Coaching Makes More Sense

Since Self-Coaching is so different from traditional therapy and other methods of self-help, I don't want you to think of it as therapy. Think of it as coaching, Self-Coaching (Self with a capital "S"). Although rooted in sound psychological and therapeutic principles, Self-Coaching is not only a totally different approach to solving problems, it's also a revolutionary new mind-set. So forget about analyzing your problems or dredging up the past in an attempt to understand why you suffer.

As I mentioned in the introduction, Self-Coaching isn't concerned with *why* you struggle. Although this notion may sound radical at first, it's no different than if you were a cigarette smoker who wanted to quit smoking. Do you really think it matters why you smoked that first cigarette? Of course not; it matters only that you break the habit. And if your goal is to create the life you want, then the only thing that matters is breaking the habits of control and insecurity that are ruining and ruling it. So, rather than finding out *why* you're insecure and struggling, Self-Coaching's five essential steps will allow you to cut to the chase by replacing "whys" with "how-tos."

A football game I played in high school can help clarify the difference between more traditional approaches to healing and the power of Self-Coaching. It was halftime and our spirits were as grim and as cold as the freezing November rain that soaked us. Losing by three touchdowns, we slumped into the locker room. Silence quickly replaced the clatter of cleats on concrete as we anticipated Coach Brown's choleric address. It started slowly, reaching fever pitch quickly as he ranted, raged, stormed, and kicked helmets with fire in his eyes. Let me tell you, it was a doozy! The mood, the atmosphere—whatever it was—shifted. Adrenaline pumping, hearts pounding, we stormed back onto the field a pack of warriors, confident, bold, and determined.

We lost that game in overtime, but compared to the defeat we were willing to accept at halftime, it was a complete and satisfying victory for me. We went out with pride and dignity. And that's exactly what a coach can accomplish. A coach lights fires, reverses negatives, defeats attitudes, and instills a can-do philosophy.

Can you imagine if a psychologist instead of a coach had addressed our team at halftime? It might have gone something like this: "Okay, boys, just settle down and reflect a moment. How does it feel to be getting your butts whipped? Go ahead, don't be afraid to let it out, we've got plenty of tissues if you're feeling upset." I don't think so! To me, when life gets bogged down with feelings of powerlessness and negativity, we don't need a stoic, reflective approach. We need an active, involved, inspirational pep talk that generates desire and demands results. We need to light the can-do fire. Whereas therapy is passive, reflective, and patient, Self-Coaching is active, involved, and, if anything, impatient. Self-Coaching's uncomplicated training program will teach you how to disarm your habits of insecurity and ineffectiveness and replace them with the tools for a successful and productive life.

Overcoming Any Problem

Over my many years of private practice I've heard just about every reason why people can't seem to find success and personal happiness. Like an echo reverberating through a tunnel, echoes of insecurity can roll through your life, distorting your every perception. Ginny, a young woman whose life had become a smorgasbord of destructiveness, will help me introduce you to how Self-Coaching approaches problems.

When I first met Ginny she was just twenty-two years old, and already her life was in danger of a total meltdown. She was a daily, addicted marijuana smoker and binge drinker who was becoming increasingly depressed and agitated. She was angry, hostile, bitter, and scared. Her home life was a shambles. Her parents were divorced. She rarely saw her father, and when she did, the potential for physical violence would quickly erupt. Her relationship with her mother was beginning to reflect this same violent loss of control, accompanied by hostility and a total lack of tolerance.

As you might imagine, Ginny's social life was terrible. It was centered mainly on finding men who would—in one way or another—finance her ability to get high. She had long ago given up on maintaining any serious relationships with her peers, and trying not to think about where she was headed, she worked hard at staying intoxicated. For Ginny, drugs and alcohol were the only escapes from an intolerable world of turmoil, confusion, and family chaos, a world where hope was replaced by a dark certainty and bitterness that there was no way out.

We talked about a trauma Ginny had recently gone through when she asked her father for money that she desperately needed to help pay for her car insurance. When her father brusquely refused, Ginny recalled feeling an intense rage that blotted out all thinking, leaving her shouting, cursing, and throwing dishes. This event was unfortunately followed by days of self-destructive behavior.

Taking the Challenge

Ginny's script read that she was destined to forever be the victim-child of a selfish and unloving father, which compelled her to keep looking for some sign of acceptance, support, possibly even love. There was a part of Ginny that just couldn't accept her father's shortcomings. How could she? If she acknowledged that her father could never give her the love she needed, then Ginny would remain incomplete. Self-Talk (the five essential steps of Self-Talk in part II will teach you this powerful technique) began to teach Ginny to start looking at her perceptions of insecurity and rejection not as givens but as habits. Ginny's habit could be stated like this: *Unless my father gives me what I need, I will never be okay. I'll always be a little girl, wanting "Daddy" to make me feel better.* Talk about feeling impotent!

Ginny didn't pursue her relationship with her father consciously. Quite the contrary. Ginny, who fancied herself as fearless, independent, and tough, almost gagged when I first suggested the concept to her. It didn't matter that Ginny was unaware of her habit of insecurity; it only mattered that it was steering her life—right into a brick wall! All this changed when she began to challenge her habit. At that point the truth was finally able to percolate to the surface. What was this truth?

Simply that she was okay—really okay! Always was. But most important, she needed to recognize that she didn't need her daddy. What she desperately needed was to experience her own maturity and power. Until now her habit of insecurity had completely obstructed this rather straightforward solution.

Keep in mind that a habit such as Ginny's isn't a deliberate, conscious decision, "Now I'm going to feel insecure." Habits of insecurity have long ago become automatic, reflexive themes that echo and repeat throughout our lives. And herein lies the biggest danger: these habits aren't going anywhere. Unless you actively challenge and break them, they can and will ruin your entire life. Like a backpack, you'll carry these habits strapped to your back for years, never realizing there's a choice.

What about you? Anything strapped to your back?

After the Choice

Self-Coaching allowed Ginny to reorient her thinking and to finally break the habits of victimization and powerlessness that had begun years before. Rather than perpetually behaving like an angry little girl looking to be rescued, Ginny instead learned to turn to herself, and that's where her power was waiting for her. Once self-doubt gets replaced with self-confidence, life begins to soar. Ginny went to rehab, stopped drinking and drugging, joined a YMCA volleyball team, and decided to go to a local community college. A recent e-mail from Ginny informed me that she's currently a solid B+ senior with high hopes of becoming a journalist. Ginny managed all the above while working at two jobs, buying a car, and starting a small investment portfolio. It's no wonder that Ginny's favorite book is Horatio Alger's *The Ragged Dick*. Talk about a rags-to-riches story!

Ginny's success may seem like an exaggeration to you, but it's not. Not when you tap into the power within you. Fortified with this instinctual reservoir of confidence and trust, no problem is insurmountable. Ginny came to me one inch away from total self-destruction. Her chaotic life contributed to her profound sense of insecurity and self-doubt. When she was high, she felt in control and invulnerable. When she was straight, she was tortured with fear, anger, low self-esteem, and distrust. Self-Coaching didn't change Ginny's external circumstances (her father still remains detached and uncaring), but by teaching her how to fight off her doubting nature and replace it with self-confidence, she was able to change her insecure thinking with the power of Self-Coaching.

Self-Coaching Reflection
If you allow insecurity to echo through your life,
don't expect to have a life.

You're going to be learning all about insecurity in chapter 3, but for now recognize that insecurity, if allowed to distort your thinking, will do one thing: it will dictate the quality of your life. And that quality will be riddled with doubt, distrust, and powerlessness. Just as you can't point one foot north and the other south and expect to begin walking, so, too, with insecurity. Part of you is pointed toward wanting a happy, effective life, and part of you is pointed toward a controlling, congested waste of a life. End result: your life becomes split and frozen with inertia.

Whether you're sixteen or sixty, emotionally stuck, suffering from inertia, worrisome anxiety, self-doubt, panic, depression, or just feeling victimized by the lack of success in your life, Self-Coaching can teach you, as it did Ginny, to reinvent your life and free yourself from the shackles of insecurity and habit that hold you prisoner. Becoming a winner isn't that complicated. In fact, with Self-Coaching's five essential steps, you'll find it's rather straightforward. If Ginny could do it, you can, too.

Transform Your Life with Two Power Words

Let's keep this simple. Two power words: "control" and "habit." Just two words—that's all you're going to need to turn your life around. Control is an attempt to manage and manipulate life because you've come to distrust your natural, spontaneous capacity to handle life. Habit refers to the specific control patterns that have become automatic, such as worrying, rumination, perfectionism, and the like. Understanding how control and habit can echo through your life is the way toward dismantling the most stubborn, resistant problems. It may sound too simplistic, or even a bit too fantastic. But that's okay. If you can accept the unobservable notion that the physical world is composed of molecules, atoms, and subatomic particles, then you should be able to accept the psychological view that everything you need to change yourself and your life, you already possess. Even if you can't observe it . . . yet.

SELF-COACHING POWER DRILL

Regardless of your current belief, periodically during each day practice allowing yourself to believe that everything you need to have a happy and successful life, you already possess. Just permit yourself to relax and accept this fundamental notion—even if it's only for a few seconds at first. Don't allow yourself to fight it. You can expect a struggle from your traditional doubts and hesitations, but for now, accept it *as if* it's true. The important thing in this drill is to begin feeling what it's like to be empowered and not victimized by life. Later, as you progress with your Self-Coaching program, you won't have struggle with this. You'll be totally convinced.

❖ ❖ ❖

2

Choosing Happiness, Dropping Misguided Goals

I don't know about you, but for me one of the most frustrating experiences in life is getting lost. A few years back, my wife, Karen, and I were headed out to California. It was August and we had just pulled into a campground north of Rapid City in the Black Hills of South Dakota. I woke up early that morning and in the muted, predawn light, noticed a distinct difference in the appearance of our tent's roof—it seemed like someone was sitting on it! Slipping out of my sleeping bag, the first thing I noticed was the chill. Dressed only in shorts and T-shirt, I wrapped a blanket around my shoulders and unzipped the tent flap. I was greeted by two things: a blast of icy cold, and at least a foot of freshly fallen snow! In August!

Bracing against the biting cold, we quickly dismantled our camp and decided to abandon our northern route—it was time to head due south, to the Grand Canyon and warmth. We left Rapid City with visions of a blazing Arizona campfire for the following night. Looking at our map, my wife noticed a diagonal road that apparently cut off about a hundred miles of cold country. My wife was all for cutting a few hours off of our trip. With some trepidation, we abandoned the interstate highway and headed due south along our newly discovered route.

After about three hours, we were puzzled about a sign that read

"Pavement Ends One Mile." Not knowing what to make of this, we assumed it was similar to signs we'd seen on the New Jersey Turnpike where road construction might last a mile or two—no big deal. Famous last words. Exactly one mile later the pavement actually ended, and we were staring at a dirt path of a road. Still optimistic that this was only an anomaly in an otherwise fine road, we continued. The snow by this time had changed over to a light rain as we were leaving the higher elevations. Along with the rain came the mud. After about an hour of slow going, I began to feel the old Ford Torino's wheels sinking, slowly at first, then more precariously. It became apparent that soon we would either have to turn back or risk getting mired down to our axles in mud. Getting out and surveying the situation, I reluctantly made my decision. Surrounded only by free-roaming cattle, no signs of civilization, our gas tank approaching the half-empty mark—we had to turn back. We made it back to Rapid City late that night, tired and defeated. After buying a catalytic heater at the local general store, we somehow managed another cold, damp evening, dreaming of places we'd rather be.

Sometimes in life it's easy to become swayed by prospects of quick routes, shortcuts, or other misguided goals. We have the illusion that because of cunning, luck, or opportunism, we might be able to figure out how to sidestep life's more traditional paths. Money, power, and status are all would-be shortcuts that promise happiness. The *illusion* of happiness, I should say. When it comes to finding out you've been headed in the wrong direction, don't go on getting deeper and deeper into problems—just get back to the main highway.

Without any long or elaborate philosophical discussions, let me introduce you to the only *highway* that really matters in life: the pursuit of happiness. It's happiness that we seek, happiness that we want, and happiness that will find you . . . if you're willing to trade control for spontaneity. The good news is that happiness is a natural, spontaneous human potential. All you need do is remove what's blocking it. Once you stop congesting your life with insecurity and control, a spontaneous and natural life-energy will introduce itself.

Defining Happiness

Success is getting what you want.
Happiness is wanting what you get.

—Dale Carnegie

For more than twenty-five years I've listened carefully to what people tell me about what they want out of life. I can say with confidence that once you eliminate misguided goals, most people are simply looking to be happy. It's not that complicated. Happiness can be defined as a state of well-being and contentment that results from living in harmony with your nature. The converse is equally true: a disjointed, unhappy life results from insecurity distorting your true nature. Happiness can be subdivided into three components:

- personal happiness
- functional happiness
- social/relationship happiness

Defining Personal Happiness: Unleashing

As Ben Franklin once said, "The Constitution only gives you the right to pursue happiness. You have to catch it." When insecurity begins steering your life, the pursuit of happiness comes to a screeching halt. There can be no real or lasting happiness when your life is driven by control. Although I agree wholeheartedly with the gist and spirit of Mr. Franklin's definition of happiness, I do, however, take issue with one word. To me, happiness isn't something you *catch* as much as something you *release*. I saw a wonderful example of this a few weeks ago.

My son Justin was dog-sitting the Labrador retriever of a friend who was visiting us from her home in New York City. Justin had removed Coby's leash and was throwing a tennis ball across our yard for her to fetch. Coby, unaccustomed to so much room, was bounding in uncontrollable bursts of speed and joy. I know dogs can't smile, but this was one happy pooch. City dogs live a life of limited instinctual opportunity. Their pleasure is dictated by the length of the leash.

Insecurity is like a leash that tethers you to a limited experience of life. Self-Coaching is your method of *unleashing* and allowing happiness to spring forward. As with Coby, once you remove the leash of insecure thinking, everything else happens very naturally. Coby didn't have to be taught how to be exuberant.

Personal happiness, living with joy and connectedness to your life, is the cornerstone of Self-Coaching. Let me tell you about Claire, a middle-aged consultant who had attended one of my book talks on Self-Coaching. Her story reflects not only the essence of personal happiness, but also the very heart and soul of Self-Coaching:

> I recall always being angry, fearful, anxious, judgmental, and so sad. I *knew* that the best part of my life was past and that my future held no riches. I couldn't imagine that I would learn the language of hope and optimism and infinite possibilities that Self-Coaching taught me. My life is good now. Every day holds promise. I know that I can make the most of whatever challenges come my way. And I am so relieved and still amazed that I can say this.
>
> It's not pleasant to remember what I was like in those days. At the time I met Dr. Luciani, I think I must have given off vibrations of distrust and criticism. I wasn't working at anything I wanted to do, I was worried about the future, afraid of my own shadow, critical of myself and my family, and unable to make simple decisions. My social life consisted of exchanging pleasantries with the mailman and giving telemarketers a hard time.
>
> I've traveled in a series of little steps and I've made myself choose unfamiliar paths just to see where they'd lead. What an adventurous thought, that I could try something without worrying about the outcome! The idea came from something Dr. Luciani said at his talk. Something about being willing to risk living my truth. I decided to try it, and the first thing I applied it to was a Chinese takeout dinner. I told myself it didn't have to be perfect, just enjoyable, and instead of my usual half

hour of agonizing, I took the risk and went with my impulse. I had never eaten a meal seasoned with a dash of liberation. It was delicious.

The next try was with a jar of my homemade blueberry jam. I wanted to give some to our new neighbors, but I didn't know whether they ate jam. And I didn't know whether one jar would seem skimpy. And I didn't know whether I'd be interrupting something if I brought it over. Or maybe I should call first, but I didn't know their number. So perhaps I should forget the whole thing. Phew! That's when I stopped my ruminations and reminded myself that it didn't have to be a perfect gesture, just a simple act of generosity. Well, I brought it over, stayed for a cup of coffee and an hour-long chat, and made a new friend.

After that it became easier to recognize the old habits of hesitation and insecurity that twisted my perceptions and held me in a vise for so long. Recognition isn't always easy to translate into action, but gradually I've learned to remind myself that I don't have to accept negativity or feelings of victimhood, that the way I see my life is the way it will be, and that if I can believe something bad, I also can believe something good!

Functional Happiness and Success

Functional happiness has to do with successful *doing*. What you do in life and how you feel about what you do often become huge stumbling blocks for many people: "But, Doctor, how can I feel successful? I'm just a stay-at-home mom." Or, "I never finished college; it's too late to get started now." And perhaps the most common lament: "My job [life, school] is so boring, I hate it!" When it comes to defining happiness, I'm sure Ann Landers or Abigail van Buren (aka Dear Abby) would agree that who you are as a person is more important than what you *do*. And I almost agree with this. I agree that who you are as a person—your self-esteem, your ability to value who you are—is an indispensable component of true and lasting happiness. But I also know that if what you do—your day-to-day work—makes you miserable, then your happiness will be compromised.

What would be a more complete definition of happiness? Self-Coaching would offer the following addendum to the above advice: Who you are as a person is more important than what you do. *And what you do in life isn't as important as how you feel about what you do.*

Allow me to elaborate. There's a legitimate human need to find meaning and expression in the things we do. This is an altogether normal and healthy desire. When we become frustrated, blocked, or otherwise prevented from finding this expression, we begin to feel unfulfilled or even depressed. Part of the problem can be blamed on how we think about success and failure. All too often we make the mistake of comparing our rather mundane, nine-to-five lives to that of the millionaire business tycoon who's chauffeured around town in a limo or to a Hollywood superstar whose second home is a villa in the south of France.

Such comparisons can—consciously or unconsciously—easily infect your life with doubts, regrets, and unrealistic expectations. After all, the paparazzi aren't following you around each day, taking photos of you doing dishes, walking the dog, or yelling at the kids (unless you're one of the Osbornes). It's this contrast that can lead you to conclude that you're stuck living a ho-hum life in a ho-hum world.

If you were to ask someone, "Which is the more important job: building a bridge or scrubbing a floor?" what do you imagine that person would tell you? You'd probably get a puzzled look and be told that building a bridge is clearly the more important job. This response would certainly represent conventional wisdom. But from a purely psychological perspective, can we really say that bridge building is more important than floor scrubbing? I say we can't, and here's why. In life, the key to happiness isn't *what* you're doing, it's what you're getting out of what you're doing. It's not about bridges or floors, it's about what that bridge or floor experience means to you.

If you're fortunate enough to have a career that resonates with your talents and needs, consider yourself blessed. I have a landscaper affectionately known as Poppy. Poppy is so connected to his work, it's hard for him to leave at the end of the day. He has to drag himself away from the project. His excitement is contagious. When he and his son Ricky show up to do some work, Poppy and I usually head off to a local rock quarry or a garden store in search of treasures. Following Poppy around a nursery is like following a child in a toy store—he can't contain himself. Poppy is connected to what he does; often he will tell me about waking at two or three in the morning with an idea or inspiration. He's an artist who expresses his soul in his planting designs. I don't know about you, but I don't know too many people like Poppy—people who are absolutely fulfilled by what they do. Most people I've met seem to be life's "plodders," another-day-another-dollar types who work for only one reason—they have to. For them getting up for work is a necessary evil, certainly not a joy.

How about you? Do you approach your days with an attitude of resignation, frustration, or despair? Sure there are reasons why you find yourself in this rut. The circumstantial demands of your life, such as putting bread on the table, paying off a car loan, saving for the kids' college fund or for your vacation next summer, can't be ignored. And maybe you've really tried to find a more satisfying job, sent out résumés, and made some phone calls, but you haven't had any luck. You feel a sense of powerlessness as you concede to the inevitable realization that, at least for the time being, you're stuck: "Hey, that's just the way it is. I've got to do what I've got to do." As one person I was working with told me, "Of course I don't like what I do. That's why they call it work, right?"

So for now, maybe you are stuck. And it may very well be that there aren't any options available. I don't dispute facts like these. What I do dispute is that you feel you have no choice. Granted, you may not have a choice jobwise, at least for the moment, but you do have a choice when it comes to living a more satisfactory life—whatever your particular job circumstance!

Conquering Boredom and Detachment

Insecurity will often create a tendency to detach from certain life challenges. This detached feeling we call boredom. So keep in mind that another word for boredom is detachment. Oftentimes, boredom—

detaching—is simply an attempt to insulate you from feelings of failure or frustration. When you're up against a situation that leaves you feeling frustrated and out of control or otherwise threatened by insecurity, your reaction may be, "I can't handle this!" Even your relationships can produce this reaction: "John isn't a very interesting person. Why waste time going to marriage counseling?" Insulation in the form of boredom-detachment, or negativity, can be just what the doctor ordered to make you feel more in control. "It doesn't bother me if I get fired. Who needs this job anyway? I'd rather be doing something more creative." Or, "No, I don't spend too much time thinking about my husband; I've got better things to do. I just wish I were married to someone else."

Please don't misunderstand. If you do happen to be stuck in a job or relationship that isn't going anywhere, I'm not opposed to your wanting a more gratifying or stimulating experience. What I am saying is that for now, whatever your current circumstance, you don't *have to* feel disconnected or bored—you have a choice! The key is learning to invest yourself in whatever you do. Whether it's chopping wood or carrying water, a personal investment of energy is what will make all the difference. In the upcoming chapters, Self-Coaching is going to teach you the specific *how-tos* involved in making this investment and transforming your life. For now, you can lay the groundwork for breaking the reflexive cycle of negativity by simply thinking about making whatever you do more meaningful. Try to attach, rather than permitting detachment to continue.

Self-Coaching Reflection
Where there's self-pride in what you do,
there can be no boredom. Only happiness.

❖ ❖ ❖

SELF-COACHING POWER DRILL

Whether it's your day-to-day job, your chores at home, or the normal demands of living, if you find yourself struggling, trying to keep your interest alive, you might want to employ this simple mantra. Whenever you find yourself bogged down, whining, or watching the clock, think: *connect rather than disconnect.* So from now on, rather than drifting off in mental reverie, choose instead to tune in, and get involved. Remember: connecting is a choice. You'll find that if you invest yourself in whatever you're doing, you'll have the antidote for boredom while simultaneously understanding how to live a more meaningful life. *Connect rather than disconnect.*

Social/Relationship Happiness

This is the last element in our happiness triad. As important as personal and functional happiness are, I feel that adequate relating and intimacy in life represents the ultimate level of integration and happiness. Humans are social beings who, given the opportunity, naturally seek to relate. Never was this point more dramatically demonstrated to me than on the morning of September 11, 2001. On that Tuesday morning, my leisurely commute to Manhattan was abruptly interrupted by a disjointed report on the radio that a plane had crashed into one of the Twin Towers—explaining the unusual plume of black smoke I had noticed when I came to the toll booths.

As I approached the George Washington Bridge, I expected long rubbernecking delays because of the unobstructed view to the Twin Towers. As predicted, the traffic came to a crawl and then to a complete stop as I reached the bridge platform. The already frantic news reports flooding the radio became absolutely hysterical as a second plane smacked into the second tower. Caught in disbelief and emotional confusion, I found myself out of my car, joining others with unbelieving eyes, all of us transfixed on that impossible, unforgettable conflagration.

Some were crying, some cursing, others were stoic with mouths agape, but all were staring at a vision of orange and black flame against an azure blue sky that our brains refused to accept. It wasn't until the South Tower collapsed that I noticed something quite startling. We all know the stereotype of New Yorkers being aloof or rude, but on this day in those frozen moments of agonizing terror, all that changed. Each one of us on that bridge inexplicably began to gravitate closer and closer toward each other rather than standing alone.

Later, just prior to our being extricated from the bridge, I noticed that my small group had become huddled together, shoulder touching shoulder. Our "home" was being violated and defiled. We, as a family, were being attacked! Our puny egos clearly couldn't handle this incomprehensible terror alone. We needed one another, and we needed to come together physically as well as emotionally. Somehow, in our instinctual selves, we knew this. Something in us was steering us, joining us together, stranger leaning against stranger.

It seems to me that, given the right circumstances, human beings naturally want to relate to one another. But if relating is so important, why does what's natural seem so . . . unnatural? The reason for this seeming paradox is that insecurity, when coupled with a kind of knee-jerk, habit thinking I call Reflexive Thinking (more about this in chapter 6), has managed to create an unnatural, solitary, controlled way of living for a lot of people. After all, relating to another human being can be risky. And for a control-oriented person, the hesitations are often deliberate: "How do I know he's not going to take advantage of me?" "What if she thinks I'm hitting on her?"

Many people who wind up in therapy have long ago substituted emotional control for legitimate relating. And in order to control emotions, feelings need to be diluted, filtered, or censored. All in an attempt to eliminate or at the very least minimize the risk of vulnerability. This filtering process creates a bottleneck kind of living where the possibility of anything more spontaneous is reserved for rare or unusual circumstances.

How do I know that relating and loving are natural? Because whenever I've seen insecurity eliminated, I've seen a more emotionally receptive attitude emerge. Every time! Once you stop controlling life, you begin to trust the truth that you can handle the vulnerability of intimacy. Clearly, this is no small demand for a lot of emotionally disengaged people. No doubt about it, risking sensitivity, intimacy, or love can challenge you in many ways. Just be forewarned: if you insist on controlling your relationships, then what you get is destined to remain a shallow facsimile of what's possible. I had a friend who jokingly echoed this sentiment: "'Tis better to have loved and lost than to have loved and won." And he was dead serious. If you avoid love—legitimate love—you will never know true happiness.

When it comes to love and intimacy, there can be many obstacles. If you maintain a controlled persona (the image you project to the world), you might feel inhibited letting your more intense, unguarded feelings be known. "I can't let him think I enjoy sex too much. What kind of girl would he think I am?" Or, "Sure I hold back; I'm not sure what would happen if I let go." When it comes to relating, fear of rejection can be a show stopper. For many, especially men, romantic and sexual performance can be a particularly sensitive and touchy subject.

Driven by media hype about such things as mutual orgasms, endless stamina, and other myths, many guys are compelled to what's often referred to as spectatoring. Rather than letting go to the intimate experience, they become caught up with insecurity, observing and evaluating their performance. This is a surefire way of stripping away the ecstatic moment and replacing it with a controlled and rigid substitute. Women, because they don't need to worry as much about the mechanics of performing as men do, are less susceptible to this type of anxiety. Less susceptible, but not immune. For them, the worries are often more about appearance than performance, and this can be just as distracting.

The bottom line: self-doubt, insecurity, and control are intimacy killers. Intimacy depends on getting out of your head and allowing—trusting—your more natural and instinctual feelings to guide you. If you find yourself observing or evaluating, then the ecstatic experience of bliss will be seriously limited. Thoughts fueled by insecurity want nothing more than to dampen any fire, convincing you that you need to "hold back" or "not get too excited."

As you now know, insecurity abhors risk; if you never risk change, insecurity owns you. In spite of your hesitations, you need to be willing to risk believing that *who* you are doesn't need to be monitored by the oppressive eye of insecurity. Once you risk trusting, then it's just a matter of letting go. Granted, if you're not used to trusting yourself (or your partner), this change in attitude may sound foolhardy, if not reckless, but it can save your relationship. So go ahead, be courageous, stop avoiding. Risk feeling what you feel—just let it happen. You're either going to find out that you're a monster who offends the world, or you're going to have a life with true intimacy and depth. As I see it, we're talking about having a life or not having one. You make the call.

One last point regarding intimacy. In a relationship, recognize that your sexual/intimate experiences reflect an accurate picture of the relationship in general. If your intimate experiences are creative and uninhibited, you are probably experiencing this same energy in the relationship. If, however, your physical relating is mechanical and inflexible, then your relationship, on some significant level, is limited by emotional control and staleness. In love and in relating, the goal is consistency. Each aspect of your relationship should reflect a natural, spontaneous expression of you and your feelings. If it doesn't, then it may be time for some Self-Coaching.

Misguided Goals: Why You're Unhappy

A rich person isn't the person who has the most,
it's the person who needs the least.

—Grandma Luciani

When it comes to defining what really matters in life, many people find themselves deceived by what I refer to as misguided goals. How do you know whether your goals are sound? Answering this question is obviously a top priority if you're going to avoid needless frustration and further loss of valuable time.

Misguided Goals: Self-Quiz

Please read the following questions carefully, but don't overthink your responses. Circle your responses as being either mostly true or mostly false as they generally pertain to your life. Answer each question even if you're not completely sure. Scoring is at the end of the test.

T F I tend to be a jealous person.

T F I often wish I felt more sure of who I am.

T F You can never have enough money.

T F I judge people by how they're dressed.

T F I can be too competitive.

T F If I'm not in charge, I'm not happy.

T F I have a tendency to bully or manipulate others.

T F I often wish I were famous.

T F I have to look better than others.

T F I'm prone to road rage.

T F It's important to have a professional/career title.

T F I have to make people respect me.

T F I fear not being successful.

T F I'm not opposed to using people to get ahead.

T F Money *can* buy happiness.

T F If it isn't the most expensive, I'd rather do without.

T F I'm willing to sacrifice most things in life to get ahead.

T F My partner's physical appearance is very important to me.

Total your "true" responses. A score of 6 or fewer suggests that you are not overly driven by misguided goals. Self-Coaching can teach you to cultivate an even deeper awareness of the goals and aspirations that are really important in your life.

A score of 7 to 12 suggests that you're moderately influenced by misguided goals. Insecurity is driving some of your perceptions and thus limiting your ultimate capacity for true satisfaction. Self-Coaching can make a noticeable difference in your overall happiness.

A score of 12 or more suggests that your goals are indeed misguided. Your life is compromised by these insecurity-driven distortions. Self-Coaching can significantly change your perspective—you're going to learn to pursue goals that offer legitimate satisfaction and happiness rather than control.

Misguided Life Goals

Life goals, like many of the concepts that you're going to be introduced to in this book, can become problems rather than solutions when driven by insecurity. Insecurity-driven goals are misguided goals that give meaning to the saying, *Be careful what you wish for, because it might come true.* Simply put, any goal that is driven by insecurity is all about control—*not* fulfillment. Although there can be an extensive array of misguided goals, I've come to recognize three major culprits:

1. Money—the accumulation of money, which is equated with security and happiness

2. Power—the quest for power and potency, which is equated with invulnerability

3. Status—the compulsion for status, which is equated with intimacy, being loved and respected

The quests for money, power, and status can all be expressed directly through your behavior. When, for example, insecurity drives your desire to own a Rolls-Royce, this behavior (owning a Rolls) can be an expression of what money can buy, a feeling of power, a status symbol, or a combination of all three. What distinguishes one insecurity-driven Rolls-Royce owner from another is what they're trying to control. Money, for example, says, *I can buy security and happiness.* Power says, *I can demand loyalty and feel invulnerable.* And status says, *I can become so important that I can make people love and respect me.*

Misguided Goal 1: Money

> *Money only appeals to selfishness and irresistibly invites abuse.*
> *Can anyone imagine Moses, Jesus, or Gandhi armed with*
> *the moneybags of Carnegie?*
>
> —Albert Einstein

Dennis, a thirty-five-year-old salesman, came to see me because he was disgruntled with life and because his lack of success was keeping him up nights. He figured that once I heard his story I'd help him figure out what was keeping him from a life of wealth and success. As it turned out, what was keeping Dennis from his goals was the square-peg-round-hole problem that's so indicative of someone chasing misguided goals—nothing in life seems like the right fit. Everything seems to fall short. It's as if life seems to abhor pursuits that are inherently valueless. End result: failure, frustration, or unhappiness. Here's what Dennis told me in our first meeting:

> I'm really getting impatient. I see other guys driving around in Mercedes, living in expensive houses, and spending the big bucks while I'm still watching every penny I spend. Ever since I was a kid, I vowed to be a millionaire when I grew up. Well, I'm grown and I've tried. Believe me, I've tried. I'm not afraid to work; in fact, that's all I do. I don't have a life, my wife is constantly complaining that she never sees me, I just don't know what else I can be doing. I see the way we're living, struggling to pay bills each month, not getting ahead. Money—all it takes is money! Take it from me, money *does* buy happiness.

Dennis isn't alone with his perception that *more is more*. He's like so many people who see money as the key to living the good life. But if you look at what Dennis is sacrificing, you have to ask, can it possibly be worth it? He's working seven days a week, goes days without ever seeing his daughter awake, his marriage is beginning to show signs of neglect and damage, and the bottom line is that he's miserable. And yet, in spite of all this, Dennis thinks he knows better—he just needs to figure out how to make more money.

How many people like Dennis do you know? People who pursue the eternal carrot—money. I was watching a documentary the other night about the wealthy residents of Palm Beach, Florida, who set—and exceed—the standard for conspicuous consumption. According to the narrator, some residents of this opulent community are living in ocean-front houses of more than sixty thousand square feet! My high school was fewer than sixty thousand square feet! What's left? After you've purchased your fourth imported luxury car, built a home that requires a road map to traverse, and vacationed at the Riviera, what in the world do you do if at this point you're still unhappy? Drugs, alcohol, divorce, depression, and suicide are no strangers to the leisure class. Quite the contrary, they seem to go along with the turf.

When I was growing up, my mother used to pray that I would never make a lot of money. She actually prayed for this! I remember feeling, *Thanks a lot, Mom!* Now I've grown to see the wisdom in her prayers. It's not that she doesn't want me to be comfortable or happy; she knows what money does to people. Smart lady.

Misguided Goal 2: Power

> *Power is the ultimate aphrodisiac.*
>
> —Henry A. Kissinger

A second misguided goal is the quest for power or potency, which is equated with invulnerability. The dictionary defines power as the ability to have control, authority, or influence over others. If you recall from our earlier discussions, insecurity has its roots in your early development. The thirst for power can have many historical sources, but typically it involves growing up in a controlling milieu where you were dominated by stronger siblings; overbearing, restrictive parents; or oppressive circumstances. Whatever the specific developmental conditions, it's safe to say that for many who struggle with low-self esteem, self-doubt, or inferiority, power can feel like a tonic. If, on the other hand, you were fortunate enough to be brought up in an environment that fostered independence and autonomy, you probably don't have a driving need to dominate or control others.

Gloria, a thirty-one-year-old embroidery factory supervisor, felt very powerful when dealing with her crew. Her motto was simple: Fear works. She knew jobs were scarce, she knew these people were unskilled laborers who were grateful to be working. And she also knew that she had the power to hire or fire.

Gloria had begun a reign of terror. She would regularly torment, threaten, and humiliate her workers. This had gone on for a few years when one day a husband of one of her "girls" came to talk to her. He told her that his wife was pregnant, that the doctor told her that she was on the verge of a nervous breakdown, and that if she didn't calm down, she could lose the baby. The man broke down and cried, pleading with Gloria to go easy on his wife.

This experience hit a chord with Gloria. Not at once, but over time she began to feel out of control, almost disoriented. She was losing her simple black-and-white approach to handling her "girls." Although she began to struggle with anxiety and depression, these weren't her problems—these were just symptoms. Her problem was her misguided desire to use power to feel less vulnerable. Until now, her power gave her the illusion that she was invulnerable, in control, and safe. As obvious as it might seem to you, it never occurred to Gloria to recognize what she had become: a coldhearted bully.

Gloria's story is an extreme example of the destructive, aphrodisiac quality that power wields. It can be a heady experience for anyone who has struggled with impotence and vulnerability. Power can manifest itself in many ways and oftentimes can be quite subtle. Perhaps you see yourself trying to control others, needing to dominate a conversation, or being a bit too bossy or competitive. If power appeals to you, if you find you have to have control over others, beware. Like Gloria, you may be living a life distorted by insecurity. And a life driven by insecurity is never a satisfying life. How can it be when your senses of happiness and well-being depend on your dominance of others?

Some other examples of power as a goal include:

- when you need to feel physically superior to others (getting into shape, learning self-defense, dieting, etc.)

- when you need to be in a position of authority or dominance over others

- when you use your education, training, or experience to dominate or bully others

- when you need to be in a position to beat others to feel good about yourself (competitive sports, advancement at work, various forms of road rage, etc.)

Misguided Goal 3: Status

The measure of a man, sir, is not in money, position, station,
or possessions. These things mean nothing. The measure of a man
is in his character, wisdom, ability, aliveness, intimacy,
creativity, courage, fearlessness, perspective, independence,
and maturity. You seem terribly impressed with the former, sir,
which suggests you are seriously lacking in the latter.

—Mark W. B. Brinton

The third and final misguided goal that I want to discuss is the compulsion for status. Whereas money is equated with buying security, and power with taking security, status has to do with winning security. The famous mythologist Joseph Campbell once told an interviewer how disturbed he was when he had asked a group of high school students what their goals were. The vast majority told him that they yearned for "name and fame." Being famous seems to have such appeal—especially for anyone who has struggled with insecurity and a sense of social anonymity. Although being famous may be a stretch for most of us, there can be different levels of fame.

Status takes on many guises. Here are a few:

- possessing objects of status: house, car, designer clothes
- superficial relationships (trophy wife or husband)
- titles (manager, president, doctor, etc.)

- insecurity-driven respect from your social group (being aggressive, intelligent, the best, etc.)

Self-Coaching Reflection
The misguided goals of money, power, and status are
all driven by insecurity. They are "outside-in" attempts
to feel more secure and in control. Only those goals
motivated by "inside-out" awareness, based on self-trust
and spontaneity, will lead to lasting happiness.

Status is like a uniform; it can be anything that brags to the world, *Hey, look at me, I'm really okay.* What about you? Are you wearing any uniforms? Trying to accumulate any medals? Do you *have* to be noticed or revered? If so, you'll be using Self-Coaching to ward off insecurity's attempt to convince you that your only chance to be happy is to build a veneer of false prominence. Status-seeking is never about status; it's about trying to compensate for your abysmal feelings of worthlessness by finding one of life's many uniforms to wear.

Money, power, status: are you caught up in these or similar illusions? If so, it's time for you to challenge these deceptions of insecurity and recognize the truth about happiness. Remember: you don't *find* happiness, you *release* it.

PART II

Your Problems:
The Roots of Change

3

Why Are You Insecure?

When I first met Anna, it was quite a shock. I was just finishing up a session when suddenly someone began pounding on my consulting room door. Startled, I threw open the door to find out what was going on. A snarling, angry woman glared back at me and said, "It's eight o'clock—time for my appointment!" With as much self-control as I could muster, I politely asked her to wait another minute while I finished up, which she grudgingly did.

When I was ready for Anna, she stormed past me into the room, red-faced and ready for a fight. I was caught off guard by this assault as she informed me that she didn't appreciate being kept waiting, and was she going to have to pay for the full hour? That was my first experience of Anna. And it didn't get much better.

I'm not sure how I managed to hold it together during those early sessions, but I did. I wasn't about to let this rude, obnoxious, fifty-two-year-old bulldozer of a woman affect me personally, even though it got very personal at times: "Did you actually pick that tie out yourself? No offense, but you don't have much taste." And after almost every sentence, Anna would demand, "Are you listening to me?" Phew! She was exhausting.

No one acts this angry, this defensive, this insensitive unless they're expecting a fight. Anna came to my office expecting a fight. She fully expected that I was going to try to manipulate her, waste her time, take her money, and leave her with more problems than when she started.

It never occurred to her that I might actually want to help her. Why would it? Everyone else in her life had made it perfectly clear that they wanted nothing to do with her. Of course, Anna had no clue why; she just wrote off this observation, insisting that she didn't need people anyway. She had her job at the courthouse, money in the bank, health insurance, and three cats. What else did she need? As far as she was concerned, this was as good as it got.

I was perplexed by Anna's assertion that her life was exactly where she wanted it. Then why had she decided to enter therapy? Reluctantly, she admitted that her boss had given her an unofficial ultimatum: get into therapy or he was going to make trouble. He told her that he was tired of everyone in the department complaining about her incorrigible, hostile attitude. Not only was I dealing with an aggressive tyrant, but now I find out she was coerced into treatment by her boss. Terrific!

Fortunately, my years of counseling experience paid off. I sensed from the start that Anna's hostility was a defense, insulation against a deeper, more profound insecurity. This insecurity prompted her to protect herself from a hostile world that wanted to hurt her. Anna's hurt-them-before-they-hurt-you attitude seemed altogether reasonable to her. It gave her the illusion that she was protected. In one sense she *was* protected—no one ever got close enough to inflict any kind of harm. No one wanted to get close to Anna!

You might suspect that I'm going to tell you about a brilliant strategy I used to diffuse Anna's hostility. Sorry. My strategy was anything but brilliant; it was downright simple. I recognized that all I had to do was not get sucked into Anna's hostility. And did it ever work! Ignoring her relentless assaults, I systematically tried to relate to her with genuine interest and concern. As you might imagine, this wasn't always easy to do.

Anna had a hard time processing my response. Growing up neglected and tormented by a depressed, alcoholic mother (who was fifteen years old when she had Anna), Anna knew only rejection. At age ten she was sent to live with an aunt who happened to be a decent woman but unfortunately was very limited in parenting skills. By this time, however, Anna's insecurity had already established itself as a habit. She was overweight, isolated, angry, detached from her peers, and constantly the target of teasing at school. You can imagine how my nontraditional, sensitive responding challenged Anna, who had no idea how to relate nondefensively. After a while I noticed that her assaults on me were diminishing. Slowly she began to relax and put her guard down. It wasn't easy for her to abandon her defenses, but once she did, things began to progress rapidly.

As Anna began to understand the implications of how insecurity was ruling her life, she was in a position to make some healthy choices: "At work today, I decided not to allow myself to imagine problems. Terry dropped something off at my desk without so much as a word. Typically I would glare at her, suspecting that her silence was a smug indication that she thought she was better than I. This time I fought off that insecurity and I actually forced myself to say, 'Thanks, Terry.' You should have seen Terry's face; she was shocked as she cautiously forced a tight-lipped smile. I'll admit it didn't feel natural, but it did feel good!"

Although Anna's in-your-face attitude may seem extreme, it clearly represents the devastating effect insecurity can have on your personality. Everyone wants to feel safe and protected in life, but if insecurity begins to distort what's dangerous and what isn't, you can find yourself in a Don Quixote–like lifestyle, seeing windmills as dragons. Anna saw dragons everywhere, no windmills. That's what insecurity does best: it makes you believe fiction rather than fact.

Getting to Know Your Root Problem

The frustrations and struggles that prevent you from having the life you want can all be traced to one root problem: insecurity. Whether you have serious problems such as anxiety or depression, or everyday skirmishes with negativity and worry, you can never overestimate the influence of insecurity. And just as any gardener will tell you how difficult it is to pull out a dandelion root, the roots of your insecurity will fight you with this same kind of resistance and tenacity. But persist you must. If you don't, then insecurity will eventually strangle your potential for a more natural, spontaneous life, just as weeds will overrun a garden.

What is insecurity? Look at some facts about it:

- Insecurity is a feeling of vulnerability and/or helplessness.
- Insecurity results from childhood psychological wounds—real or imagined.
- Insecurity is the false belief that you can't handle life or some aspect of life.
- Ongoing insecurity is based on distortions of reality, not fact.
- Insecurity becomes a habit of thinking and perceiving.
- Insecurity minimizes the possibility for accurate self-perception.
- Over time, insecurity feels like a natural part of your personality.
- Insecurity becomes worse over time.
- Like any habit, the habit of insecurity can be broken.

Let's take a moment to appraise your general level of insecurity—your root system.

Insecurity Self-Quiz

Please read the following questions carefully, but don't overthink your responses. Circle your responses as being either mostly true or mostly false as they generally pertain to your life. Answer each question even if you're not completely sure. Scoring is at the end of the test.

T	F	I tend to be shy or uneasy with strangers.
T	F	I'd rather be at home than going out on an adventure.
T	F	I wish I were smarter.
T	F	I never have enough money.
T	F	I'm usually pessimistic.

T   F   I often wish I were better looking.

T   F   I don't think I'm as good as others.

T   F   If people know the real me, they would think differently.

T   F   In relationships, I tend to cling.

T   F   If someone's quiet, I might think they're angry.

T   F   I'm usually afraid to get too close to others.

T   F   I would be a lot happier if I didn't worry so much.

T   F   I have lots of fears.

T   F   I tend to hide my feelings.

T   F   In relationships, I tend to get hostile.

T   F   I often wonder what people *really* think of me.

T   F   I find it hard to trust.

T   F   I worry about my looks.

T   F   I have a hard time saying no.

T   F   I tend to be too sensitive.

T   F   I'm overly cautious.

T   F   I worry about getting sick.

T   F   I often feel guilty.

T   F   I hate the way I look in pictures.

T   F   I don't think of myself as an emotionally strong person.

A score of 1 to 10 "true" answers indicates a tolerable degree of insecurity. You'll be using this book more for personality expansion rather than for repair.

A score of 11 to 16 "true" answers indicates a moderate level of insecurity. Insecurity is probably undermining your capacity for effective and successful living. You can expect this book to significantly change your view and experience of the world.

If you scored 17 or more "true" answers, you may be suffering substantial interference due to insecurity. Your self-worth and confidence have been eroded by insecurity, and it's clear you're going to need to restructure your thoughts and perceptions.

Nature plus Nurture

I was giving a talk recently where I mentioned that no one is born insecure, it's something you learn. During the question-and-answer period a rather upset mother challenged me on this notion. "You can't tell me that children aren't born insecure," she said. "I can see it in my own children. My youngest has always been shy, less willing to try new things, and fearful. He didn't learn this, he has always been this way." This mother's observation seems consistent with what most people feel about children. Go to any playground and you'll see leaders, followers, criers, whiners, sulkers, and loners. Clearly, children seem to be disposed toward certain tendencies, but are any of these tendencies synonymous with insecurity? To answer this seeming paradox you must understand the difference between an insecurity and a disposition.

I define a disposition as a genetic tendency toward certain physical or psychological traits. You can have a disposition toward alcohol, obesity, music, art, mathematics, athletics, introversion, or extroversion, but unless a tendency (disposition) is embraced and reinforced, it won't necessarily manifest itself.

Take the case of Matt. He didn't consciously embrace his disposition toward obesity, but his stubborn refusal to see the truth cost him a relationship.

As far back as Matt could remember, he struggled with his weight and his lack of self-confidence. At twenty-nine years old, Matt met a woman and had his first intimate relationship. Unfortunately, his insecurity precluded any possibility of love developing. The early years of taunting and teasing had left their mark, and Matt was intensely insecure about his weight. Now, as an adult, he unconsciously allowed his insecurity to define his self-worth. Although only moderately overweight all his life, Matt saw himself as totally repulsive. Still, in spite of his self-disgust, the relationship did progress—for a while. But unfortunately Matt's anxiety grew until he finally decided he had to end the relationship.

Matt's story demonstrates how a disposition—his physical propensity toward being overweight—can become inadvertently infused with primitive, childlike associations of insecurity. When Matt looked at himself through the haze of insecurity, he decided that no one would or could want him. It mattered little that someone *did* want him; he wasn't about to let himself risk believing this. His girlfriend pleaded, but Matt remained resolute. He knew that one day she would become revolted by his obesity. Matt's insecurity spoke, and he listened. The self-flagellation led to a cycle of isolation and emotional abuse, oftentimes culminating in reckless bingeing and drinking. Weight loss wasn't an option for Matt; he had already concluded that his fate was sealed and unalterable (even though his diet was atrocious and the only exercise he got was climbing his steps). It wasn't obesity that was steering Matt's life, it was his insecurity—his "yes-but" deflections and childish insistence on burying his head in the sand and avoiding life.

Self-Coaching Reflection
A genetic disposition may influence your life,
but it's not a life sentence.

When it comes to our struggles in life, there are many reasons why we don't fight back. One of the biggest is the misguided notion that who we are is an unalterable consequence of our "genetic personality." There is no such thing as a genetically determined personality. Sure, your personality is *influenced* by your genetic disposition, but it's not *determined* by it! My nieces Chrissy and Kathy are identical twins who share many wonderful personality traits. They're two generous, compassionate, outgoing, friendly, terrific people, but in many ways they're quite different. Here's a list they compiled for me:

Chrissy	Kathy
Neat	Sloppy
Aggressive	Passive
Impatient	Patient
On the go	Homebody
Self-conscious	Secure
Saver	Spender

Chrissy and Kathy share an identical genetic disposition, which means they started life with exactly the same equipment. They grew up together, same parents, same schools, yet, as you can see, their personalities are anything but identical. How can this be? The only reasonable answer is to conclude that our genetic disposition must interact with our unique experiences growing up (and our interpretation of these experiences).

genetic disposition + unique life experiences = adult personality

Imagine a husband and wife going on a vacation to Mexico, each equipped with the same camera, both sharing the same experience. Their photos after the vacation might give two totally different views of this experience. The husband's pictures might, for example, include numerous pictures of Mayan ruins and wildlife, giving an impression of a wilderness adventure. The wife's pictures, on the other hand, might include many pictures of the local shops and culture, capturing more of the local charm and quaint lifestyle. Same cameras, different foci. It's not your camera that determines what pictures you take. Similarly, it's not your disposition that determines whether you are a success or a failure.

So if we eliminate the effects of genetics, fate, and karma, what can we blame our misguided lives on? I suspect you already know my answer: insecurity. It's insecurity that's steering your life, not you. The question remains: how do we become insecure in the first place? Insecurity can be an end result of early traumatic experiences, but more often it's a by-product of faulty misperceptions. Children grow up in a world that requires constant assimilation and interpretation. Their security is dependent not only on the quality of the parenting they receive (and there are no perfect parents), but also on the serendipity of their life experiences. Since children are limited by their immaturity, faulty conclusions are certainly not unusual. Let me share one such misinterpretation in my early life that generated a considerable amount of insecurity. You'd never think a simple birds-and-bees talk would set the stage for insecurity, but for me it did.

How to Avoid Eternal Damnation

Back in my early days of innocence, I attended a small Catholic school in northern New Jersey. I remember the day clearly: it was a bucolic spring day, and a scent of lilac was drifting into the open awning windows of my seventh-grade classroom. I was startled out of a deep reverie when the boys in our class were told to meet with Father Divine in the cafeteria. Never before had we been separated from the girls; something big was about to happen. Nervously, we took our seats while Father Divine stood silent and looming at a prominently placed podium, validating my anticipation that something very weighty was about to happen.

I don't remember exactly what Father Divine said that day, but I do recall the following, almost word for word: "Boys, tonight and every night, I want you to remember when you go to bed to make sure your hands are on top of the covers. Remember, if your hands are under the covers, this is an occasion for sin"—but all that I remembered as I walked home that day, reviewing the good father's admonition, was that one word: "sin." Why in the world it was a sin to have my hands under the covers was a complete mystery to me, but then again much of what I learned about sin and hellfire and all that was quite a jumble. Long ago I decided to stop trying to figure out how to save my soul and just do as I was told.

I was confident that first night. After all, it seemed like a no-brainer: hands on top of the covers, no sin; hands under the covers, sin. You weren't going to get me to burn in hell for all eternity for something so simple as sleeping with my hands on top of the covers. Confidently I drifted off to sleep. At one point during that first night I awoke to find one hand under the covers! A bit unnerved by this inadvertent transgression, I once again positioned my hand. Have you ever tried to monitor your hands during the night? I did, and let me tell you, it drove me crazy. I guess over time I did manage to train myself to prefer the safe, hands-on-top-of-covers position, but let me tell you, for months I struggled with the fear of not being able to control and protect my eternal soul.

Call me naive, call me unconscious, but it wasn't until I was twenty-four years old that one night I happened to wake up (hands on top of the covers, of course) with the startling realization of just what Father Divine was talking about, only this time I remembered the complete phrase: "occasion for sin"! All these years I thought it was just one more dictum of the Catholic Church, one more rule. Never in my wildest imagination did I ever associate this "sin" with anything so—so obvious! To be honest, I'm not sure whether it would have made me less or more anxious if I had known the intent of Father Divine's talk that day. I only know that my misperception had complicated my world and made me more aware of just how vulnerable I was. I mean, I couldn't even protect my eternal soul! For a young, sensitive, thoroughly suggestible kid, this was big-time insecurity, and I began to lose confidence in my ability to steer my life away from sin.

It wasn't Father Divine's fault, nor was it the fault of the Catholic Church for trying to impart its view of morality. The problem was my misinterpretation, and herein lies the problem. All kids try to make sense of information that is often lacking or fragmented. Most of the time there is little fallout. Occasionally, like with my bedtime surveillance, faulty interpretation can lead to self-doubt, fear, and unrealistic expectations. And since insecurity is an altogether ubiquitous outcome of growing up, to a greater or lesser extent, it's unavoidable. But the unfortunate truth is that insecurity isn't something we simply outgrow. Velcro-like, it clings to us and accumulates throughout our life.

It's for this reason that a Self-Coaching approach is necessary to release you from the habits that have overrun your life. Understanding a habit isn't enough; breaking a habit is all that counts. Just as Anna, mentioned at the beginning of this chapter, found out, you have to go against what feels natural and insist on making the healthier choices.

The truth of the matter is that your insecurity, laid down years ago, has now come to feel natural, like a part of you. Breaking free and establishing self-trust and confidence will, at first, feel totally unnatural. Expect that you will fight this feeling. Your reaction might be "It's just not me, I can't do that." But don't be fooled this time.

SELF-COACHING POWER DRILL

Take a moment to reflect. Find one thing that you feel insecure about. It can be anything: your appearance, being rejected, making mistakes, wasting time—whatever makes you feel uneasy, doubtful, or anxious. Once you focus on this insecurity, recognize how natural it feels, how identified you are with it, and how reflexive it has become. Using this same focused consciousness, try to understand that what you feel just isn't true; it's part of the distortion perpetrated by insecurity. With this in mind, take the plunge and see if you can go against insecurity's propaganda. See if you can, for example, allow yourself to waste time without feeling guilty. Or perhaps go to the store even if your hair isn't perfect. Or admit that you're wrong without feeling inferior. See if you, rather than your insecurity, can call the shots. Regardless of how intimidated or fearful you may feel, try. Every effort is a building experience that will serve you as you progress with your Self-Coaching program.

❖ ❖ ❖

Positioning Yourself

By taking the time now to understand your struggle from the root up, you begin to position yourself for Self-Coaching's five essential steps to creating the life you want. It might help to see insecurity as the motor, and your compliance—in word, thought, and deed—as the fuel that keeps the motor going. To cut off the fuel supply you're going to need a firm foundation of understanding combined with the coaching that will convince you to risk going for it.

4

Choose Not to Worry

Years ago, when I was in high school, I recall an incident where I had been worrying about something, got distracted, and forgot what I was worrying about. My mother, seeing my scrunched-up face, asked what was wrong. "I can't remember what I was worrying about," I replied. She then said, "Well, if you can't remember, then it couldn't have been that important." Sure, easy for her to say! Ignoring my mother's seemingly inane advice, I went on for most of that morning trying to backtrack my thoughts. For whatever compulsive reason, I felt I had to pin this one down. After all, what if it was important? How could I be so reckless to just forget about it? Finally, by lunchtime, it came back to me: I had been worrying about wasting time!

The irony of this revelation didn't escape me, even at the ripe old age of sixteen. My insight may have been influenced by a short story called "The Beast in the Jungle," by Henry James, which we had been reading that same week in English class. If you're prone to worry, I highly recommend that you read this engaging story about a man who has a premonition of a terrible calamity that will one day destroy his life. This is no ordinary premonition; it completely devours his life. In the end, it's not a beast from a jungle that winds up destroying him, it's the realization that his life had been needlessly sacrificed to worry and rumination. A beast nevertheless!

What about you? Is worry devouring and wasting away your life?

Stop Feeding the Pigeons

You're now going to learn how to conquer what most feel is an unconquerable part of life: worrying. More than any other psychological stumbling block, nothing causes more turbulence and distress in our lives than worry. When it comes to a life of struggle, worry is usually a ubiquitous component. For some it's debilitating, chronic worry and rumination about anything and everything, while for others it's more situation-specific: "I just cracked my tooth. What if I have to have a root canal?" Regardless of whether you're a chronic worrier (a worrywart) or a casual, part-time worrier, worry is a big problem because it's the primary source of nourishment for your insecurity. Let me explain.

Imagine that every morning you go out on your deck and manage to spend a leisurely half hour relaxing and enjoying the paper. One morning you go out and notice a few pigeons milling about, pecking and minding their own business. Enjoying their company, you remember to bring out a handful of bread crumbs the next morning to throw to the birds. Within a few days, you're inundated with hundreds of pigeons, leaving your once-pristine deck world a shambles of feathers, droppings, and mayhem.

You come to me and ask, "Dr. Joe, what am I to do?" I ask one question: "Are you still feeding the pigeons?" "Well, yes," you answer innocently. Incredulously, I respond, "Then STOP feeding the pigeons!" If you worry, you're feeding the pigeons of insecurity. And if you insist on feeding your insecurity, then the distasteful truth is that you'll wind up with the tormented life you deserve.

If you find yourself in a hole, stop digging.

—Will Rogers

Isn't Worry a Normal Part of Life?

Remember the sixties song "War"? The first verse goes, *War, what is it good for? Absolutely nothing!* That's how I'd like to begin this chapter: *Worry, what is it good for? Absolutely nothing!* By the end of this chapter you'll be humming this tune.

"I have worried about thousands of things in my life, most of which never happened," said Mark Twain. How many things have you worried about in your life? Forget your life; how many things have you worried about today? Most people will tell you they wish they didn't worry so much, but what can you do—worrying is a part of life, right? Sure, worry is a part of life, but is it a natural part? What about healthy?

Take the following self-quiz to help you assess your worry quotient.

Worry Self-Quiz

The following questions are geared to help you assess whether you are a worrier. Please read the questions carefully, but don't overthink your responses. Circle your responses as being either mostly true or mostly false as they generally pertain to your life. Answer each question even if you're not completely sure. Scoring is at the end of the test.

T	F	My mind usually races from thought to thought when I'm trying to fall asleep.
T	F	I get very upset when things go wrong.
T	F	I can't stand it when someone's mad at me.
T	F	I often feel guilty.
T	F	I often start my sentences "What if . . ."
T	F	I hate to be unprepared.
T	F	I think too much.
T	F	I'm usually tense.
T	F	Concern about money is always an issue with me.
T	F	The news gets me too upset.
T	F	I'm too cautious.
T	F	When something upsets me, I can't let it go.
T	F	I feel uneasy when someone else drives.
T	F	I don't like flying.

T	F	I don't feel safe.
T	F	I second-guess everything I do.
T	F	I'm a pessimist.
T	F	I'm overly concerned about my health.
T	F	I rarely take risks; I'd rather be safe than sorry.
T	F	I have lots of fears.
T	F	Terrorism is often on my mind.
T	F	I usually try to anticipate what's going to happen.
T	F	When in conflict, I usually try to figure out the worst-case scenario.
T	F	I'm the kind of person who's always waiting for that other shoe to drop—always waiting for something to go wrong.

Total your "true" responses. A score of 9 or fewer suggests that you are not overly burdened with worry. Self-Coaching can teach you to cultivate an even deeper sense of self-trust and spontaneity.

A score of 10 to 15 suggests that you're a moderate worrier. For you, worry may be a limiting aspect of your life. Self-Coaching can make a noticeable difference in your overall feeling of well-being and sense of personal security.

A score of 16 or more suggests that worrying is a significant stressor in your day-to-day experience. For you, life is compromised by an attempt to maintain control by worrying or ruminating. Self-Coaching is going to change your perspective. Rather than trying to anticipate life, you're going to learn to live more spontaneously.

Concern vs. Worry

Everyone worries, right? Worrying is so common, you might be tempted to think of it as an instinct. And if it's instinctual, then it must be an adaptive part of our nature. Worrying about saber-toothed tigers while traipsing through the primeval jungles certainly would have provided a distinct survival advantage to our ancestors. Yet, as convincing as this speculation may seem, I assure you, worrying didn't serve our ancestors back on the African savanna, nor does it serve you today sitting at your desk in a high-rise office building.

To understand why worrying, as a strategy, is counterproductive, you'll need to understand the difference between being worried and being concerned. Worry is the incessant, ruminative speculation of what might go wrong—an anticipation of chaos. This can be because of a past mishap: *What if I insulted her? She may bad-mouth me at work,* or because of a mishap that's waiting to happen: *What if I don't find an apartment? Then what will I do?* It's a form of self-torment, best described as *what-if* thinking.

Concern, on the other hand, is a calculated consideration and assessment of actual danger. Whereas worrying anticipates problems and things going awry (loss of control), concern is more fact-based and geared toward problem-solving. What do you think serves you when facing a life challenge: dealing with fact (being concerned), or dealing with fiction (worrying)?

Read through the examples below and ask yourself if there is *any* advantage to worrying:

Worry: What if I can't fit into that dress?
Concern: I'm going to have to watch what I eat if I'm going to fit into that dress.

Worry: What if I'm late?
Concern: I'd better leave fifteen minutes earlier to avoid construction delays.

Worry: What if she says no?
Concern: Whether she says yes or no, either way, I'll survive.

Worry: This is a strange pain. What if it's serious?
Concern: If I'm uncomfortable tomorrow, I'll call the doctor. No sense assuming the worst.

As you can see from the examples above, if you compare worry with concern, there's no contest—not if you want to be effective. Being concerned is an adaptive and constructive way of thinking that really prepares you for life's challenges. Being worried, on the other hand, is a circular, destructive kind of thinking that leads to a life of stress, anxiety, or panic.

There is worry and there is concern. Concern is circumstance-driven; worry is insecurity-driven. Worry, insecurity-driven—from the inside out—is bad for you. Concern, circumstance-driven—from the outside in—is good for you.

Worry

- insecurity-driven—from the inside out
- subjective concern over what can go wrong
- dealing with fiction (i.e., what-if thinking)
- highly emotional, regardless of the circumstance
- counterproductive, psychologically destructive

Concern

- circumstance-driven—from the outside in
- objective concern over a life challenge
- dealing with fact
- emotions proportionate to circumstance
- constructive

I believe that we are equipped with a natural inclination not for worrying, but for being concerned when life challenges us. Problems arise when our natural tendency to be concerned becomes degraded by the introduction of insecurity, turning it into a habit of worry. The equation looks like this:

$$concern + insecurity = worry$$

The Worry Scam

Worrying may not be natural or instinctual, but it certainly is popular. How do we explain this popularity? There must be something compelling about worry that attracts so many devotees. And there is. When confronted with uncertainties in life, worry gives the illusion of control. This is particularly appealing for someone who is already insecure and struggling with fears. The scam goes like this: *If I worry, I can anticipate what's going to happen, and if I can be rehearsed and braced, then I'll be less vulnerable.* Doesn't sound so bad, being braced and prepared for confrontation, right? But let's not overlook something that every worrywart already knows: worry begets worry. Worry doesn't solve anything; it opens the floodgates to more worry, more doubt, and lots more stress. The bottom line: worry isn't what it's cracked up to be. Rather than preparing and protecting you, it actually diminishes your capacity for effective living.

Worry: Friend or Foe?

Worry is an attempt to counteract your perceived shortcomings. Since insecurity leaves you feeling ill equipped to handle what life throws at you, worry gives you the illusion that in spite of feeling powerless, you're actually doing *something* about your plight! On the surface you think that worrying is going reduce your vulnerability by preparing or bracing you for what's coming—hey, at least it's something! And something is better than nothing. You're only worrying because you want to feel safe. So what's the big deal? As we've discussed, worry isn't an effective problem-solver. In fact, worry is a problem-maker! And that *is* a big deal.

Phil, a forty-year-old unemployed chef who was allowing worry to devour him, will serve as an example and a preview of how Self-Coaching can help:

> I'm forty years old, I've got a ton of bills, and absolutely no prospects. My wife and I barely talk anymore. I don't even care about going to my daughter's basketball games. I'm embarrassed to run into anyone because they'll ask if I'm working yet. I'm overweight, I worry about having a heart attack, I'm tired all the time,

my stomach is constantly in knots—I'm just a wreck. You know what the worst part of all this is? It's that things are only going to get worse. This economy is bad and it's not going to get better. Then what?

What does a forty-year-old, unemployed, second-rate chef do for a living? I'm too old to change careers, I don't even know what else I could do. I'm not a good student, I have no interests, I really can't do anything else. What's going to happen? I can't fall asleep at night; my thoughts are beginning to scare me. I've lost all my confidence, not that I was ever that confident. I've always been a worrier, but now it's ridiculous. I'm afraid to make any decision. I never imagined I'd be out of work this long. What if I can't find work? What will I do? One thing this has taught me: in this world, nothing is safe. Nothing! I must have been in never-never land, because I never saw this coming. And it's only going to get worse.

No doubt about it, Phil is caught up in a cycle of worry and fear. Considering his distressing circumstances, you could ask whether Phil really has a choice. If you were confronted with a similar crisis, wouldn't you worry, too? Is it plausible or even fair to expect that when clobbered by life you can choose not to be victimized by worry and fear? Contrary to what you might feel, the answer is yes, it is both plausible and fair!

Looking at Phil's dilemma, you can see that what upsets him are his dark, insecurity-driven prognostications about the future.

Self-Coaching Reflection
Worry is the habit of anticipating chaos.

For starters, Phil needs to recognize the difference between being concerned and being worried. This would allow him to begin shifting his focus to facts rather than the fictions he was conjuring up. And for Phil or for you, if you worry, this simple shift in thinking can make all the difference in the world. Granted, if you live on this planet, you're not going to eliminate bad things from happening. But what you can eliminate is the needless debilitation caused by worrying. I stand firmly by what I said earlier in this chapter: *Worry, what is it good for? Absolutely nothing!*

Self-Coaching Reflection
Worry is the child of desperation.

What Serves Me, What Hurts Me

According to our popular Groundhog Day myth, if the groundhog, affectionately called Punxsutawney Phil, emerges from his hole and sees the sun, he regards this as a bad omen. Predicting six more weeks of bad weather, Phil returns to his hole. The Phil in our story is another kind of groundhog, who, when faced with his worries and perceived bad omens, retreats from life, seeking short-term protection. But remember, Phil can't avoid his life forever. Eventually he's got to poke his head out.

Phil needed to lick his wounds and begin the long struggle back to self-respect and confidence. In the months that followed being fired, Phil struggled with his reflexive, groundhog worrying. The first Self-Coaching challenge was to convince Phil that beating himself up, hiding from life, and worrying weren't serving him. Whenever he found himself caught up in a mental struggle, I encouraged Phil to ask: "Do these thoughts *serve* me or do they *hurt* me?" Just asking this question was enough to raise his consciousness so that he no longer would be blindly driven by his insecurity. And by embracing a what-serves-me, what-hurts-me attitude, Phil was on his way to relinquishing his role of victim. It clearly didn't serve him to become more dysfunctional, to harbor self-doubt, or to insist that he was a victim.

❖ ❖ ❖

SELF-COACHING POWER DRILL

The technique Phil used—*what serves me, what hurts me*—deserves a closer look. Worriers typically are so caught up in their habit of anticipating chaos that there is a noticeable lack of consciousness (as you will see in chapter 6, this is the trademark of Reflexive Thinking in general). And when left unattended, habits will roll along willy-nilly throughout your life, doing their damage. This happens because they aren't scrutinized. The simple act of scrutiny, asking, *does this serve me or does this hurt me,* forces a light of consciousness to be cast on the habit. Habits seem to prefer the dark; once exposed, they begin to wilt. I suggest that you begin to incorporate this simple scrutiny to any worry thought. You might be surprised at how silly worry can be once you expose it.

Reactive Rather Than Proactive

Rather than spending each day mired in a black-and-white, anticipatory world of worry, where the only thing that mattered was finding a job, I suggested to Phil that he consider living more courageously—in the moment. He was all ears as I explained an experiment I wanted him to try. I wanted Phil to get out of his head, to step apart from his typical harangue of worrisome prognostications, and instead of squeezing himself, insisting on figuring everything out, to simply let his day unfold. Specifically, I wanted him to be more *reactive* rather than *proactive*. Instead of inventing things to worry about, to just respond to whatever was happening in real time. This was an alien concept for him (as it is for most worriers), and would obviously require a willingness to risk being vulnerable (actually, not *being* vulnerable, just *feeling* more vulnerable). Since worriers live mainly in the future with their what-iffing, living in the present can be quite a challenge.

The only instruction I gave Phil was to wake up each morning and try—in any way he could—to get out of his head and then to simply let life unfold. (Note: Phil was already introduced to Self-Talk's five steps and had several tools at his disposal for accomplishing this task.) This was especially important when pursuing the serendipitous mechanics—

phone calls, reading the want ads, sending out résumés, and so on—involved in looking for a job. The key was to begin discrediting his worrisome, future-oriented attempts to control life and just focus on the actual—and factual—chores of the day. I made it clear to Phil that we weren't trying to get him to *stop* thinking; that's not possible. What we were trying to do was shift his usual, anticipatory-worry thinking to a more reactive, here-and-now kind of thinking. Although pessimistic, he was eager to see if anything would happen if he allowed his life to unfold more naturally rather than from his head.

Since Phil confessed to being a lifelong worrywart, he quickly found out that *being reactive* was a lot easier said than done—but not impossible. Although he was finally beginning to see the bigger picture regarding his cycle of worry (i.e., his loss of confidence and inability to trust life along with his desire to control outcomes), his dependency on worry as a form of control had grown so strong that discarding it for such a vague alternative as living in the moment at first seemed downright reckless. Nevertheless, Phil knew he needed to break from tradition. His insecurity was killing him! Pain can be a great motivator.

Getting Off the Island

If you're a worrier, then like Phil, getting out of your overthinking head and living reactively in the moment will require significant effort along with a willingness to believe that there's more to life than simply what's roiling about in your mind. Think of the ego as a speck, a pinpoint of an island in a vast ocean. The island represents ego consciousness—the part of your thinking that is observable. Aside from normal thinking, the ego is also the locus of all reflexive, insecurity-driven thinking. The ocean, on the other hand, represents the unlimited resources of the Self—the part of your thinking that is not subject to direct observation. This is the realm of instinct, intuition, and whim.

Worrywarts live exclusively on their little islands. And just as you would know every nook and cranny of a tiny island if you were shipwrecked, worrywarts know only one circumscribed existence, one universe, one way, characterized by fretting, anticipating, and what-iffing. For the worrier, thoughts are treated as facts: "What, are you crazy? You want me to go on that interview and wing it? You must be out of your mind. I've got to prepare! I've got to give this some thought." For worrywarts, the ocean remains a vast, frightening expanse of unexplored potential. Yet contained in those depths is unlimited power and potential for liberated, courageous living.

Using Self-Talk's five steps, Phil stumbled a bit at first and needed to become more disciplined in his efforts, but after a few modest successes, he was off to the races: "My head doesn't feel like it's going to explode anymore. My mind has actually quieted down. I'm letting life come to me rather than my dictating every move and every thought. I keep telling myself, tomorrow will take care of itself. I've got to tell you, being reactive is the only way to go."

Phil was right. When he began to step out of the shadow of reflexive worrying, things simply began to fall into place more naturally and effortlessly. Amazingly, "tomorrow" did just seem to take care of itself. Through a neighbor's contact, Phil eventually landed a job in a rather posh New York restaurant. In the ensuing months he was trained by one of the best pastry chefs in the city and eventually moved on to one of the most reputable hotels in Manhattan. Obviously Phil never considered this outcome in his initial worries—his crystal ball was too clouded with worry, doubt, doom, and gloom. Worry only sees things going wrong. Never the complete picture. And certainly never anything optimistic.

Worriers Are Overthinkers and Self-Hypnotists

Ever notice how silly someone else's worry seems to you? How many times have you told someone to stop making mountains out of molehills? Unfortunately, if worry has become your reflex, mountain-making is what you do best. And when you're making mountains, the strangest things can seem very real. Insecurity is, first and foremost, opportunistic. Give it an opening and it will take you for a ride.

A few years back, I used to teach abnormal psychology. As was always the case, after my lecture on neurosis and psychosis, I would receive urgent requests from students who had inexplicably "come down" with neurotic or psychotic symptoms. These were the worriers, the overthinkers who were susceptible to taking a suggestion, implanting it in their minds—"I could be paranoid. I do feel persecuted!"— and then opening the floodgates to worry, anxiety, and panic.

If you're prone to overthinking and generating worry and anxiety in your life, then it's imperative for you to recognize the enormous power of the mind. When I was studying hypnosis in graduate school, I remember seeing a training film where a subject was induced into a deep state of hypnosis. While the subject was in this state, the hypnotist told him that he was going to burn his hand with a cigarette. The hypnotist touched the subject's hand with an ice cube. The subject winced, as if actually touched by a cigarette, but what was remarkable was that the spot where the ice cube touched formed a welt! What we tell ourselves and what we believe make all the difference. If you implant a bit of suggestion (self-hypnosis) in your mind and you believe it, you will live that suggestion.

Relativity

In writing this chapter, I've come to realize the powerful and caustic influence that worry has on our well-being. One thing I would like you to do: Remind yourself of the countless problems and worries that have come and gone in your life. How many problems have you solved to date? One thousand? Fifty thousand? Somehow you've managed to survive, to figure out, solve, get around, under, or over every obstacle. Right? Every crisis eventually becomes history and you move on. What makes you think that today's worries will be any different?

5

Stop Controlling Life

No one likes feeling out of control—least of all me! A few years ago I had been vacationing at the Jersey shore and was out one morning in a rented rowboat doing some fluke fishing. Had I been situated differently in the boat, I may have noticed a wall of black weather bearing down on me like a freight train. By the time I eventually shifted my position and witnessed the storm, it was too late. Dropping my fishing gear, I frantically pulled up the anchor and turned my attention to starting the small outboard motor.

Adrenaline surging, I frantically pulled the starter cord, desperately trying to maintain my balance as my small aluminum craft was tossed about by angry, froth-tipped waves. Finally the motor responded. Scanning the horizon, the nearest shore seemed to be about a mile to my east. At full throttle I headed for the bouncing horizon. Unfortunately, the waves and wind made it impossible to make headway. Turning back, I saw the black curtain of rain no more than fifty feet away! Seconds later the rain reached me. As the winds picked up I was greeted with one more ominous problem: lightning!

The lightning filled the sky around me with crackling, deafening explosions. I'm not a seasoned boater, nor am I well versed on the habits of lightning, but it occurred to me that I was the highest point for about one square mile! On some primal level, I knew I had to do something quickly. Fortunately, one nautical fact floated back to me in those tumultuous moments: Barganet Bay's average depth is eighteen inches! I had to get off my perch in order to lower my chances of becoming a lightning rod. Squinting against the pelting rain, I found the anchor, tossed it overboard, and jumped into the bay, which, fortunately, was only thigh deep. Somehow in the blinding fury of the storm, I noticed, not more than a few yards away, a bed of seaweed and mud. Without contemplation, I dove headlong into it.

Heart pounding, fear pulsing through my body, I somehow managed to snuggle into the mud . . . and my fate. It wasn't long before I realized I wasn't alone! I was so numbed by the elements and chaos that at first I hadn't noticed a piercing pain in my toe. Finally reaching for my food, I was greeted with a rather formidable blue crab clutching onto my toe with, I'm sure, nefarious intentions. After extricating my toe from the pincers, I became aware of other crabs milling about. For the next few minutes I was engaged in a writhing dance with my tormentors—at least it distracted me from the storm, which was now mercifully passing. But not without one ear-splitting crack of lightning that hit my boat!

The storm left me as it had reached me—a receding black curtain of rain, taking its wrath eastward. The absence of rain, wind, and waves was immediate. I stood up in the brilliant sunlight, toe bleeding but otherwise no worse for the wear.

Sure, it was my survival instinct that took over that day, but saying it differently, I was out of control, and everything in me was fighting to regain control and survive. Depending on the crisis (or interpretation of the crisis) we respond with a powerful, instinctual urge to maintain control and avoid calamity. It's human nature. My instincts told me that unless I gained control, the only thing left at the end of the day would be the tattered remains of a small rowboat along with the tattered remains of Joe Luciani.

Whether it be surviving a storm, lowering your cholesterol, or driving on an icy road, there's no debate that your desire and instinct for being in control can save your life. And because being in control is such a necessary part of survival, it often blinds us to another form of control that isn't at all beneficial. In fact, the desire for control, when driven by insecurity rather than life circumstances, is *the* reason why your life has deteriorated.

When, because of insecurity, your life is driven by control, you become susceptible to depression, anxiety, hostility, or ineffectiveness. The symptoms aren't what really matter, but the cause does: attempting to control—rather than live—your life. To me, this concept of control is nothing less than psychology's grand unifying theory. And in my many years of practice, it's this concept, more than any other, that has consistently allowed me to treat and eliminate the most stubborn of problems. I recognize that this is a radical assertion, but I have become convinced that no matter what your symptoms, no matter how minor or severe, once you realize it's all about trying to control life, you will never be confused again. You'll see.

Good Control, Bad Control

For the record, let me reassert that there's nothing wrong with wanting to be in control. When the doctor tells you your blood pressure is elevated and you decide to watch what you eat, that's taking control, and that's smart. When the forecast is for snow and you decide not to wear your best shoes, that's also smart. But when you stay up nights ruminating (turning things over and over in your mind) that your five-year-old may never go to an Ivy League school, well, that's insecurity! There are two kinds of control: one I call circumstance-driven control, and the other I call insecurity-driven control.

Circumstance-driven control is an attempt to respond to real and objective life circumstances with appropriate and proportionate responses. If your job is in danger, figuring out how not to displease your boss is an example of circumstance-driven control. Likewise, if you're overweight, watching what you eat and exercising a flabby body is also an example of responding to real and objective life circumstances. Circumstance-driven control is not only normal and smart, it's probably instinctual.

I've heard it said that the fundamental driving biological force is the avoidance of pain and the seeking of pleasure. I have no problem with this. However, I feel there is another, more compelling argument to define human nature: maintaining control.

77

From the time we are born, humans demonstrate an abhorrence for feeling out of control. For a brief period in the first few months of an infant's life if, for example, you were to simulate a falling motion (i.e., loss of control) by lowering the child quickly, the baby will fling out his or her arms sideways, palms up and thumbs flexed, followed by a pulling or clasping of the arms close to the chest. This is called the Moro reflex, and it's been suggested that this reflex may be an evolutionary hanger-on from when our more primordial ancestors carried their young in trees. When the infant experiences a loss of control (falling), the instinct is to regain control (clinging to the mother). Control. It's what makes us feel safe and secure in an oftentimes inhospitable world.

My storm experience mentioned above is a clear example of a circumstance-driven need for control. Being caught in a squall in the middle of a bay is one circumstance that demands a controlling response—if you want to live to write about it. There's a second form of control, which, instead of being driven by external circumstances, is driven by inner thoughts and perceptions. This form of control I call insecurity-driven control. Insecurity-driven control has less to do with actual, external events and everything to do with our "interpretation" of these events. If, for example, you wear suspenders because you feel your perfectly good belt may break, and then begin worrying whether your suspenders will carry the load in the event of a belt failure, this is insecurity-driven control. It has nothing to do with your belt and everything to do with your insecure what-iffing. What matters is whether the danger is from within or from without.

Let's compare the two types of reactions. If you're with a friend and that friend becomes inexplicably quiet and detached, you may ask, "What's wrong?" In this case you're responding to a circumstance-driven desire for control—an explanation of this unusual shift in your friend's demeanor. If, on the other hand, you see your friend pull away and you begin to worry, *What's going on? What did I say? I must have hurt her feelings!* this form of trying to "figure out" is also an attempt to be in control, but it's driven by your insecurities and self-doubts. You're convinced that if only you can figure out what you did wrong, then you can be braced and ready to defend yourself. It's based on the assumption that you did something wrong. No evidence, just your assumption, driven by your insecurity.

Circumstance-Driven Control	Insecurity-Driven Control
Dictated by external events (e.g., bringing an umbrella to work on a cloudy day or taking medicine when you're sick)	Dictated by internal events (e.g., misperceptions, fear, doubt, worry)
Control that's generated from the outside in	Control that's generated from the inside out

Worry, rumination, perfectionism, doubt, fear, avoidance, even hostility, can all be insecurity-driven attempts to control life. In the chapters that follow I will be going into these different controlling strategies in more depth. For now, keep in mind that if you've lost faith in yourself or in life itself, you're probably feeling vulnerable and out of control.

One question: when you're feeling out of control, what do you do? If you're at all insecure, you probably seek more control. And then more and more. An insecurity-driven life of control quickly becomes a dog-chasing-its-tail existence: the more control you have, the more you need. Why? Because insecurity-driven control isn't a solution, it's actually part of the problem! A problem that began at some time in your life when you were wounded in such a way that your basic sense of security was undermined. And without self-trust, a compensatory life of control becomes inevitable. Self-Coaching is going to teach you that there's only one path leading to success and solace. It's not the path of rigidity and control, but of living life spontaneously with a renewed sense of trust.

Does This Sound like You?

Before explaining this life strategy of control further and perhaps prejudicing your responses, take a short self-test to determine your control tendencies. Please read the following questions carefully, but don't overthink your responses. Circle your responses as being either mostly true or mostly false as they generally pertain to your life. Answer each question even if you're not completely sure. Scoring is at the end of the test.

Self-Quiz: Control Tendencies

T   F   Once I start something, I can't relax until it's done.

T   F   When things go wrong, I usually get upset.

T   F   I worry a lot.

T   F   If my desk is a mess, I can't get any work done.

T   F   When something sounds too good to be true, it usually is.

T   F   I try to be prepared for whatever might happen.

T   F   It's important that other people like me.

T   F   People take advantage of me.

T   F   I always have a good reason for what I do.

T   F   I don't take criticism well.

T   F   I rarely feel I'm wrong.

T   F   I typically respond to criticism with a "yes, but" response.

T   F   I usually find it hard to be on time.

T   F   I'm impatient with others' mistakes.

T   F   I like to be the one driving the car.

T   F   I often have trouble making decisions.

T   F   I want what I want when I want it.

T   F   I'm too vulnerable.

T   F   Most people can't be trusted.

T	F	I'm always in my head, figuring, thinking, ruminating, and so on.
T	F	I prefer knowing what's ahead than being surprised.
T	F	Once I make up my mind, I don't change it easily.
T	F	I tend to be black or white in my thinking.
T	F	I've been accused of being inflexible or too rigid.
T	F	I like to have the last word in any argument.
T	F	I have perfectionistic tendencies.
T	F	At times I can be compulsively driven.
T	F	I would call myself an overthinker.

Total your "true" responses. A score of 10 or fewer suggests that you are not an overly controlling person. Self-Coaching can teach you to cultivate an even deeper sense of self-trust and spontaneity.

A score of 11 to 17 suggests that you are a moderately controlling person. For you, the need for control is a limiting factor in your life. Self-Coaching can make a noticeable difference in your overall feeling of well-being and sense of personal security.

A score of 17 or more suggests that you are a particularly controlling person. For you, life is significantly compromised by a need to maintain control. Self-Coaching is going to change your perspective. You don't need more control; you need more self-trust.

Holding Back Your Ocean

In the previous chapter we discussed how insecurity is the root responsible for your faltering life. If insecurity is the root, then trying to control life is the weed that grows from it. A desire to control life may begin subtly, going unnoticed for years, with no ill effects. But make no mistake: in time, control will act like a weed, overrunning your life with worry, doubt, and fear. Trying to control life is such a destructive strategy, yet few people see it for what it is.

Part of the problem is that control has so many faces, so many expressions, it's easy to be fooled. Power, money, status, perfectionism, worry, and rumination are just a few potential examples of this altogether pervasive by-product of insecurity. Any of these controlling expressions may seem to serve you for a time, but eventually, rather than serving you, they begin to own you. You cling more and more to these destructive strategies, trying desperately to stem the tide of insecurity. I remember when I was a child playing in the sand at the ocean. I spent most of the day building a magnificent sand castle and, as the incoming tide approached, frantically began to throw together a sand barrier to try to protect my creation. Excused only by my immaturity, I actually thought I could save my castle. But after all, I was only a child.

What's your excuse? Do you actually think you can go on controlling life indefinitely? Forestalling or preventing bad things from happening? If not prevent, perhaps manage to avoid all conflict? If so, how long do you imagine that you can you hold back your ocean? Certainly not forever. And that's why you're beginning to suffer, because the ocean of anxiety, insecurity, and self-doubt is beginning to encroach on your protected ego castle.

To create the life you want, realize that the answer you seek can't be found in holding life back—this has become the problem. To get to this answer, we begin with a question: why have you become one of control's victims?

How to Be Miserable

Controlling life gives you an artificial and temporary feeling of security—you get seduced into thinking that your particular juggle of controlling strategies will last forever. Kim managed to go twenty-eight years before colliding with the myth that life can be controlled.

Kim came to our first session confused. She thought she had chosen the life she wanted. "Ever since I was a kid, I've always wanted to be a teacher. Now that I'm finally there, I'm getting crippled with panic attacks!" It didn't make any sense to Kim, and I must admit that when we first met, it didn't make much sense to me either. Historically, she told me about a white-picket-fence-childhood with loving parents and siblings—even an affectionate dog named Fluffy. Kim was always a star performer, extolled by both teachers and friends alike. Shortly after high school she married her high school sweetheart, and insists it still feels as if she's on her honeymoon. She began attending night school, earning a teaching degree after six years. During this time, Kim described herself as secure, confident, and not prone to worry. Why in the world would this woman, for no apparent reason, be suffering from panic attacks that were beginning to sabotage her new teaching job? I felt sure I was missing something. I was.

What Kim had left out was the fact that her rather compulsive father had brought her up not only to seek excellence but also to demand it. He praised her to the hilt for success and would withdraw in obvious disappointment in what Kim remembered as "my letting him down." From these early shaping experiences, Kim had learned her lesson very well: "'Tis better to succeed." She demanded perfection in everything she did. For example, she readily admitted that she wasn't the brightest student in her class, but she was the most tenacious, always finding a way to get that A (and nothing less than an A). Kim's dream was to be a teacher, and she never once doubted that one day she would make a *perfect* teacher.

Her first teaching job was in an inner-city school in upper Manhattan. Kim quickly found herself in an unusual predicament—her charm, work ethic, and personality didn't produce the results she expected. The kids weren't that bad—considering the intimidating security presence and lockdown nature of the school—but for Kim, her classroom wasn't reflecting the degree of control and competence she was used to. Uncharacteristically, she began to worry. *What if the principal walks in and sees them out of their seats? What if I can't control them?* Kim tried harder to reach her students, she tried to be more entertaining, tried being more creative, even tried pleading, but nothing worked. Her students were out of control, but more important, it was Kim who was feeling out of control. Her long run of trying to juggle control was about to end.

When we first started talking, Kim had no clue why she was having panic attacks. Sure, her job was stressful, but she had handled stress before without panicking. Panic and anxiety had never given her a problem before, so what was different now? What was different was that Kim's traditional control tactics weren't working anymore. Her usual controlling strategy of being the pleaser, the star, or the performer didn't work at this school, and Kim was left without the ability to ensure, much less "demand," her success. Stripped of her ability to manipulate and steer others according to her needs, she felt vulnerable, powerless, and out of control—the quintessential formula for panic attacks. Until now, Kim had never faced a life circumstance that refused to conform to her will—but now she had twenty-one reasons to panic. Twenty-one children who refused to allow Kim's illusion of control to go on.

Without going into a long discussion of Kim's rather short-term treatment, I'll just say that all Kim needed was to see that as long as she insisted on a life of control, she was inadvertently insisting that anything less than perfect was intolerable. When her students presented her with a dose of "imperfect" reality, *panic* was another word for "I can't handle this!" The truth was that Kim was more than capable of being a completely competent teacher. The problem was that she had never learned to trust her abilities. How could she? She had always been too distracted trying to perfect her controlling strategies.

On the surface, Kim's story may seem unrelated to your struggles, but a deeper look at how these early habits are formed might reveal some useful insights into your personal control system. At a very young age, wanting to please her father, Kim inadvertently found that certain behaviors always brought praise. These behaviors were connected with being the "star" and not making mistakes. Rather than living spontaneously, reacting to situations naturally, Kim instead began anticipating and calculating life. The reason this lifestyle became her habit was simple: it worked! The only problem was that the more Kim worked at figuring life out, the less she learned to live life in a more trusting, instinctual way.

Your Battle Persona

Children don't have many resources to use when they feel unsafe or insecure, so it's natural for them, when threatened, to try to find control and safety anywhere they can. That's what kids do; they find ways—although quite primitive—to regain control. Some, like Kim, mentioned earlier, try to become so perfect that there won't be any criticism. Others may become shy, hypersensitive worriers, attempting to sniff out danger before it arrives, while others may find that tantrums can eventually coerce the world into compliance. Whatever works is likely to reduce tension and anxiety and be tried again. And again. These strategies of defense and control laid down in your childhood eventually shape what might be referred to as your battle persona.

Since insecurity is an inescapable human experience, Self-Coaching will teach you to assess where you've insulated yourself with strategies of control. Regardless of how attached you've become to your strategies or identified with your battle persona, invariably a life of control guarantees only one thing: you'll be pulled away from your true source of strength and vitality. How many times in your life have you heard someone say, "Just be yourself, you'll do much better"? This happens to be one of life's bigger truths, but so many people have become deluded into thinking that control is the glue keeping life from crumbling that they don't have a clue what "being yourself" means anymore. If you recall, Kim didn't have a clue until she took the risk of finding out what would happen when she stopped trying to control everyone. She learned to pay less attention to the fears and doubts that filled her head and instead allowed herself (through her Self-Coaching training) to become more reactive and spontaneous. She didn't try to control by rehearsing or anticipating, she simply allowed herself to trust her more spontaneous instinctual abilities. At first she expected the world to end without control, but she found that her world didn't end, it began!

If your life has become victimized by control, you're probably no stranger to frustration, failure, even anxiety or depression. And yet what have you done about it? Worried more? Become more perfectionistic? Had a few extra glasses of wine each night? Has your battle persona become hardened by convictions of impotence and fear? And if while reading these words, you just found yourself thinking, *Yes, but . . .*, please read on. The quality of your life may depend on it.

Self-Coaching Reflection
If your healthy instincts are sacrificed to a life of control, sooner or later you will suffer.

Our humanness can be traced back millions of years ago to the African savanna. During our long evolutionary development, we humans have acquired many instincts, intuitions, and other survival skills. But rather than trusting these innate, spontaneous abilities to react and respond to life, we've become indoctrinated by control's dictum: *figure life out first, then react.* You don't have to look any further to find out why we've become a society of overthinkers.

Recalling an image from a previous chapter, if the ocean is seen as a repository for all of our instinctual-survival nature, then normal ego consciousness is only a tiny island within this vast ocean. A person addicted to control sees just the opposite. He or she sees control as the dominant, protective force in life—the ocean. And herein lies the problem. When our natural, boundless ability to live our lives is subordinated by the rigid narrow-mindedness of control, we begin to lose our instinctual, spontaneous capacity for handling life. Instead we wind up overloading ourselves with the demands that control imposes, such as worrying, rumination, perfectionism, fear, and so on. This overload eventually wears us down. It's like a motor without oil: friction will cause it to smoke, then to grind, and eventually—inevitably—the motor will stop running.

What about you? Notice any smoke yet? For you this friction might take the form of anxiety or irritability, perhaps just a vague knot in your stomach every day as you go to work. Or maybe you have just lost interest in sexually relating to your husband. If you see smoke in the form of psychological friction, you need to stop overloading. You need to start, right now, learning that control is the cause of friction in your life. The goal is to eliminate control from your life and let your natural instincts and intuitions provide the lubrication for an effortless ride.

Control: Crazy as a Fox

Once you begin to open the door to your truth (rather than control's distortions), you are ready—really ready—to change your life. Although change is always possible, sometimes changing who or what you are feels downright impossible. Don't be duped by this perception. The truth is that change may *feel* impossible, but it's not! And if there's one thing I know about feelings, it's that they can be very convincing— as well as very deceptive. Just ask Christine—she felt she was crazy! Little did she realize that feeling crazy was her unique way of feeling in control.

When Christine was born, her mother went through a severe post-partum depression and had to be separated from Christine for the first two years of her life. When Christine was four, her father died suddenly of a heart attack. Then, when Christine was fifteen, her mother died of cancer, leaving her to live with her two well-intentioned but grossly inadequate older brothers.

Christine's traumatic past never gave her an adequate foundation of love and security (her root system of insecurity). This became blatantly evident toward the end of her teen years, when her behavior began to deteriorate. She began to worry and obsess about everything—her looks, her friends, what she said, what she didn't say (all controlling strategies). She would ruminate, sometimes for days, over her insecurity-driven perceptions: *What if she thinks I'm selfish? I was so nervous, I'm not sure what I said. Maybe she thinks I'm crazy. Maybe she's going to tell her friends about me. What will they think? Maybe . . .* Christine's insecurity also showed in her erratic socializations. Her friends, unable to interpret her unpredictable behavior, began to pull away. Of course, Christine interpreted this as proof positive that her misgivings and fears were indeed true. She *was* crazy.

What else could explain why she had no friends? To Christine it was obvious. She felt she was crazy, and everyone she knew seemed to agree. By throwing up her hands with this admission, she felt a strange sense of relief. Let's face it: if you're crazy, you're excused from life, you don't have to take responsibility for your behavior. And if you're not responsible for anything you say or do, then you're insulated from any would-be attack or criticism. You're in control.

When I met Christine she was thirty and had long ago accepted her fate: "Everyone knows I'm crazy! I can't help it, I just keep doing crazy things. I don't care anymore, I don't want to live. Even my psychiatrist told me I'm not normal!" Initially she entered therapy because one of her brothers had come across my earlier book on Self-Coaching and felt that was exactly what his sister needed. Christine was less than enthusiastic about our meeting. She had been to too many therapists and psychiatrists to have any optimism about one more psychologist. In her mind, I was just one more shrink who would lead to one more disappointment.

Looking for That Spark

Initially, Christine's attendance was erratic, but she did manage to string together enough sessions to get a hint of my approach. In spite of her conviction of "why bother, what's the use?" something seemed to ignite as she became guardedly interested in this new approach called Self-Coaching. From Christine, any interest in anything was a major coup. You might wonder why, considering the insulating effects of her control strategies, she would be interested in changing. The answer to this is important. Regardless of how effective your control strategies may be, they require a lot of effort. Eventually you become depleted maintaining them.

Christine was depleted, tired, depressed, and longing for a life that she felt was impossible. Impossible, but only because she was buying the fiction that she was crazy. Keep in mind that your desire for a more natural, spontaneous, effective life can get suppressed, but it can never be extinguished. There was a part of Christine that knew this, the part of her that perked up when she heard about this new option called Self-Coaching.

Although her behavior was, to be honest, quite strange, I immediately realized that what was strange was the fact that she was acting, literally, like a child. She spoke in a kind of whiny, mousy voice, never making eye contact, often getting into ridiculous tantrums, and sulking about how therapy and life were just too hard for her. I struggled in these early sessions. Could it possibly be that what I was seeing was nothing more than a practiced and profound habit of immaturity?

❖ ❖ ❖

SELF-COACHING POWER DRILL

It's important for me to share with you a technique that has never failed me in therapy. Whenever I'm trying to sift through the chaos of what I'm presented with, I always ask myself, "How is this related to control?" In Christine's case I concluded that being a child offered her control by excusing her from the responsibility of being an adult. It mattered little that her life was in chaos; it only mattered that she felt insulated from her fear of a greater danger—handling life. As I've said repeatedly: control distorts reality. As you sift through the struggle and confusion of your life, get used to always asking, "How are my symptoms related to control?" You will find, as I have time and time again, that the formula works—all struggle can be related to control!

❖ ❖ ❖

Standing Up to Control

I began by systematically challenging Christine's controlling perception that she was crazy and therefore excused from any of life's responsibilities. Because of her profound insecurity, Christine's choices were limited. She could risk handling life, which seemed impossible considering her low degree of self-trust, or find a way to avoid risking by being crazy. One of the first things I did was limit her daily hysterical phone calls. Reflexively, she was conditioned to look to everyone else for answers—everyone but herself. I needed her to understand that as long as she insisted that I had the answers, she would never build up her own self-confidence. "My job isn't giving you fish, It's teaching you how to fish," I glibly told Christine one day.

"I hate fish!" she responded. "I don't know what to do! Don't you understand? I can't stop this pain! What's wrong with you? Why won't you tell me? What kind of a psychologist are you?"

I stood my ground, explaining to Christine that she already possessed everything she needed for healing. Like muscles that had atrophied, her security and confidence needed to be exercised and challenged. Most important, Christine needed to know that her insistence that she couldn't handle life was not true. Reluctantly, she began to accept the fact that I wasn't going to return her hysterical phone demands. She had no choice but to live with her tantrums. Or abandon them.

After about a month of "muscle-building," it happened. Christine finally saw a glimpse of her truth. The lightbulb went on and she actually lit up. Her eyes wide, a smile on her face, energy in her voice, she reported to me that she had had a revelation. She recognized that she had been acting "mental" all these years because it felt safer than trying to handle life and facing failure.

I explained to her that just as the sun prevents us from seeing the stars during the day, her feelings of self-loathing and insecurity had blinded her from seeing the truth about her personality. It wasn't that she couldn't handle life, it was that her insecurity blinded her from knowing that she could.

Using the various techniques that you will be learning shortly, Christine began to challenge the fictions that, until now, had seemed so real to her. Slowly at first, something began to stir. Christine began, for the first time in her life, to see things more clearly. She began to challenge the insecurity-contaminated fears and doubts that ruled her life. Once challenged, these fictions quickly began to evaporate. The more she realized the truth of her life—that she wasn't crazy, that she was, in fact, quite sane—the more empowered she became.

Christine began working more and more at a bakery until she was working every day. She began to go to a gym and started to look different. I must admit, her first impression—head held down, eyes darting from side to side, scanning for danger—did leave the impression that something was very wrong. In fact, the first day she drove alone to my office, someone called the police because this "strange" woman was slowly driving up and down the block looking altogether suspicious.

I wish you could see Christine now. Her head is always held high, a smile brings out features that were dormant for most of her life, and her makeup accentuates her blue eyes. She's dating, going back to school, and well, let's just say that Christine has found Christine—a more mature Christine. This mature potential was always there; unfortunately it had become eclipsed by her habits of insecurity and control. One thing is for sure: Christine has learned firsthand how deceptive feelings can be.

Christine's story is extreme, but it demonstrates the terrible effects that control can have not only on shaping your personality, but also on your ability to choose the life you want.

Juggling

Years ago my father taught me to juggle. The way to do it is to hold two balls in one hand, throw one straight up, and then with a curving motion, throw the second ball while the first is beginning to fall—throw, catch, throw. Okay, now we move to the big time: three-ball juggling. The essential requirement of three-ball juggling is to get one ball suspended in air, midway between your hands. A circular motion of both hands, releasing and catching, is necessary. I can't help you with four-ball juggling because I never had the patience to learn the more complicated movements required. But, as adept as I am with three-ball juggling, occasionally things go awry. I've had oranges smash into walls; balls crash into valued objects; and once, trying to impress my daughter, I even tried three small pumpkins. When the first crashed midair into the second, well, let's just say that when a juggled pumpkin collapses, it can be a messy thing. Ask my daughter.

The reason juggling is hard is because it defies nature. Those balls are just looking for an excuse to obey the demands of gravity. When you try to control life you're defying nature, what I call the natural law of psychological spontaneity. Psychological spontaneity is learning to live life reactively, in the moment, rather than abstractly, from the head, anticipating some future event—one that may or may not occur.

So if you're invited to go to a party, the key isn't figuring out if you'll have a good time, it's to show up and just let the party unfold. To do this requires a leap of faith—Self-Coaching is going to teach you how to leap—as you tell yourself that whatever happens, you'll handle it. Done. Issued closed. No more debate. If someone insults you, you'll react; if you get bored, you'll survive. What you're not going to do is indulge your habit of doubt, trying to figure all this out before you ring the doorbell!

When you can't trust yourself to handle life, you're not going to risk living spontaneously. That would require a willingness to believe that whatever you do or say will be appropriate and self-enhancing. But when insecurity diminishes self-trust, you're not interested in taking any chances—the only thing you can do is eliminate risk and stop feeling out of control. And how have you typically done this? Control. It all boils down to control.

What makes control so seemingly irresistible is the misguided notion that if you work hard enough, you can actually control fate: *Will I have a good time at the party? What if . . . ?* Charles, a young, energetic electrician I had begun working with, was telling me about a trip he was planning to Atlantic City. Ever since his last trip to the casino, he had been figuring out how to beat a particular slot machine. It was a machine where you could increase your bet anywhere from ten to thirty dollars. He had it all figured out, something with the number of times the bars would show up in relation to some other symbol—trust me, it was an elaborate scheme that Charles was sure would yield riches.

The week after Charles's trip to Atlantic City, he came to his session and reluctantly told me how he had taken the long walk to the ATM machine four times to replenish his cash. He wound up losing three thousand dollars. When I asked about his scheme, he told me that he hadn't given up, he had to make a few adjustments, and as soon as he accumulated more money, he was planning a return visit to win back his money. Like the slots at Atlantic City, insecurity has a way of always beating you. Maybe not at first, but give it time. And like Charles, you just keep going back for more control, convinced that your jackpot of happiness depends on it.

The opposite of control is risk. No doubt about it: if you're insecure, trying to control life seems a lot safer than risking spontaneity. After all, if you're not prepared, how will you be able to handle life's challenges? You'll try any strategy that seems to offer control and insulation from life's doubts, won't you? Whereas a secure person with trust will say, *Guess I'll find out if Sue really loves me when I pop the question,* an insecure person without self-trust needs to anticipate what's coming: *What if she rejects me? What will I say? What if she's not sure? What if . . . ?*

You Do the Math

There are many controlling strategies, each of which can be visualized as the balls that comprise a juggle. A juggle that, unbeknownst to you, you've been practicing and perfecting all your life. *What-iffing,* for example, can be one of the balls you rely on to anticipate (and control) problems. Another choice might be *have-tos,* compulsive attempts to eliminate problems. Maybe you're a *yes, but* person, always excusing yourself from responsibility with rationalizations. The number of balls (strategies of control) you juggle is unique to you. Some people manage with a few balls, while others have a vast arsenal.

Since you're reading this book, I'm going to assume that your life isn't where you want it to be. Whatever your expectations, hopes, or desires, you just haven't been successful enough. But how could this be? You try so hard. You see successful, happy people all around you. Why them and not you? Wasn't the purpose (conscious or unconscious) of your juggle to sidestep life's problems and figure out how to get to that brass ring? So why are you so miserable? Where's *your* brass ring? It just doesn't seem to add up.

Controlling life doesn't add up—and it won't add up—because rather than addition, control subtracts. The reality is that any activity that goes against nature creates friction. Psychological friction not only subtracts from life, but also eventually wears you down to a point of ineffectiveness, mishap, or collapse. Controlling life goes against nature because, as I said in a previous chapter, controlling life is a myth. The objective truth is that life cannot be controlled.

Are You Up to the Challenge?

Even with insight and awareness, there may still be a moment of hesitation before you're convinced to pull the trigger on your slumping life. This apprehension is normal. It occurs when you recognize that without your defensive juggle *and* without a capacity for legitimate self-trust, you really are naked and vulnerable. For this one brief and scary moment in your life, you'll have to tolerate standing strong while I ask one thing of you: resist the temptation to pick up the scattered balls of control. Self-Coaching can't help you if you're too busy attending to your juggle—too busy responding to the fictions inspired by your insecurity. I'm going to ask you to take the risk, go ahead, allow yourself to be naked and vulnerable, just long enough to see the truth. Once you do, you won't need my encouragement.

6

Reflexive Thinking

My daughter has just begun driving. I empathize with her struggle. Nothing is natural. She has to think about everything: *Am I going too fast? Should I start turning now? Am I too close to that other car?* Her driving is all being handled on a conscious, intellectual level. In a few months all this will change. I, on the other hand, have been driving for decades. I learned to drive my father's 1955 Chevy in my backyard. How I didn't burn out his clutch shifting from first to second gear, slamming on the brakes at the end of the driveway, and then throwing it into reverse, I'll never know. It still amazes me how the complex process of driving a stick shift can become totally automatic.

Just last week, my wife asked me why, when I drive, it never feels like a smooth ride. I thought about this and noticed that at various points during acceleration, on some reflexive level, it was as if I were driving my father's old '55 Chevy! I would ease up on the gas, hesitate—seemingly going through the motion of shifting gears—then resume giving the gas, resulting in my wife's warranted criticism. Amazing how old reflexes can follow us around.

Whatever the activity—driving a car, swinging a golf club, or learning office etiquette—what at first takes effort and consciousness can, over time and with practice, become completely automatic. When our behavior shifts from conscious to automatic, we say it has become a reflex or a habit. Certain habits and reflexes, such as touch-typing at your keyboard or riding a bicycle, demonstrate the value of not having to relearn and figure out a task every time we encounter it. There's no doubt that with certain behaviors, reflexive living is a definite advantage. Could you imagine getting behind the wheel of your car every day without these reflexes? *Let's see, key goes in the ignition. Okay, turn it to the right, put the lever into drive, press the accelerator . . . is that too much? Am I going too fast?* The capacity for automatic, less-than-conscious living can make for a much more efficient way of life.

When Thinking Becomes Reflexive

Most helpful reflexes, such as driving your car or dialing a familiar phone number, don't require any formal thinking—you just react automatically with very little formal cognition. This type of thinking might best be described as *autothinking*. There's another type of automatic responding that isn't at all efficient. Or helpful. In fact, it's downright destructive. It's a type of thinking that hammers you with doubts, fears, and worries. This type of thinking I call Reflexive Thinking, which describes older, more primitive thinking habits that are insecurity-driven and destructive.

Essentially what I'm describing are two types of habits. The first type—the autothinking type—includes habits such as nail biting; slouching; playing with your hair; forgetting to take your elbow off the table; or, in my case, unconsciously shifting gears and driving my wife crazy. These habits aren't necessarily connected to any detailed thinking and may best be described as knee-jerk, nonthinking reflexes. When we talk about a habit, this is typically what most people think of—habits that are mostly automatic and typically devoid of any formal thinking.

The second type of habit—the Reflexive Thinking type—might be expressed as a tendency toward self-doubt, pessimism, or certain fears—psychological habits that are driven by insecurity. Reflexive Thinking is usually expressed through destructive, repetitive themes that run through your life. For example, "I can't do that, it's too hard, I don't care if everyone criticizes. I'm just not good enough." Or, "Nope, I don't have a choice. I have to be perfect." This type of reflex totally depends on negative thoughts to feed it and keep it alive.

Understanding Reflexive Thinking will help you figure out why your life has stalled and why the same old problems just seem to keep repeating themselves. Why you've become so ineffective and powerless.

When Insecurity Dictates

Today you are the sum total of the habits of your life. When you look at your life frozen in the moment, you're not just looking at a here-and-now snapshot, you're also looking at the culmination of everything that preceded this moment. The ups and downs of your life, the illnesses, separations, traumas, surprises, successes, failures, and accidents, all adding up to yield this moment, the person you've become. And the one crucial, architectural force behind all these formative shaping experiences has been your experience of insecurity.

If insecurity is the driving force behind your Reflexive Thinking habits, then you might, for example, find yourself with compulsive habits, things that you *have to* do rather than *want to* do. Or perhaps you have a habit of worry—a chronic what-iffing reflex. Such long-standing habits may seem totally natural, part of who you are. But just because something *seems* natural doesn't mean it *is* natural. What's truly natural in life flows effortlessly from us; it builds us and restores us. This is a creative force, what the biologists call anabolic energy. There is another kind of energy—the energy mandated by insecurity. This energy—catabolic energy—requires effort, maintenance, and stamina.

Self-Coaching Reflection
All Reflexive Thinking is catabolic.

Reflexive Thinking—catabolic thinking—depletes you rather than restores you. This psychological depletion need not always be dramatic or even obvious, but make no mistake—it is cumulative and it will catch up with you. Once depleted, you become the proverbial accident waiting to happen. And while you're waiting for the crash, your life begins to sputter and stall.

For example, Carrie, a twenty-nine-year-old veterinarian, thought she could hide the fact that she was insecure, until one day her reflexive, catabolic energy finally caught up with her. She found herself unable to finish an operation on a German shepherd because of a panic attack. Andy, a forty-year-old plumber, is another example of the cumulative effects of Reflexive Thinking. At first his shyness around people was more of an annoyance than a problem. But as time went on he began to find it more and more difficult to deal with his customers. When he found himself unable to return their phone calls and watched his business begin to crumble, he knew he had a big problem—a catabolic one.

The following are examples of anabolic and catabolic Reflexive Thinking choices. See if any of these describe you:

Anabolic: Listening to music
Catabolic: Always on the go—never time to relax

Anabolic: Enjoying having friends visit
Catabolic: Performing rather than relating to others; preferring to be alone

Anabolic: Meditation, prayer, or contemplation to relax
Catabolic: Relax only when distracted by externals (TV, alcohol, competition, etc.)

Anabolic: Enjoying success
Catabolic: Never feeling satisfied with success

Anabolic: Artistic pursuits—process-oriented choices
Catabolic: Being or demanding perfection—goal-oriented choices

Anabolic: Relishing happy times
Catabolic: Never being happy enough

Anabolic: Healthy, moderate living
Catabolic: Excessive exercise to lose weight and stay healthy, or excessive indulgences such as drinking, eating, or smoking

Anabolic: Trusting your decisions
Catabolic: Feeling guilty or doubtful about your decisions

Anabolic: No problem handling commitments such as relationships, appointments, being on time
Catabolic: Problems with commitment: difficulty with intimacy, always late for appointments, always rushing

If any of the catabolic examples apply to you, you need to be aware that there is a psychological chafing going on that diminishes the quality of your life. Self-Coaching is an anabolic program for learning to restore rather than exhaust your life.

Knee-Jerk Living

Reflexive Thinking isn't thinking in the usual sense, it's more of a prepackaged, repetitive script driven by insecurity. The focus of your Reflexive Thinking may shift over time. When you were younger, perhaps you worried incessantly about your looks. Now there's been a shift as you've come to worry more about money and security, paying less attention to the ten extra pounds you've put on. The focus may shift, but your script remains the same: self-doubt, distrust, and a lot of what-iffing. Saying it differently, it's not about specifics like how your hair looks, or whether you have enough money in the bank; it's about whether you feel you're in control. The bottom line: attempting to control life will inevitably lead to Reflexive Thinking, which leads to knee-jerk living.

Since Reflexive Thinking has its origins in your formative years, it typically retains a distinctive childlike flavor. Because of this immaturity—so typical of Reflexive Thinking—I referred to this concept in my previous book, *Self-Coaching: How to Heal Anxiety and Depression,* as the voice of the Insecure Child. Now I want to refine and broaden this concept, since while the concept of the Insecure Child is helpful to many people, it can be the source of some confusion as well. By referring to insecurity-driven thinking as Reflexive Thinking, I'm describing the process of destructive, insecure thinking rather than simply labeling it. (In the interest of not throwing out the *Insecure Child* with the bathwater, where this concept can offer specific insight or clarity, I will use it sparingly.)

Self-Coaching Reflection
When insecurity goes unchallenged, the slide toward
Reflexive Thinking is inevitable.

❖ ❖ ❖

SELF-COACHING POWER DRILL

Here's a useful tool: whenever you find yourself agitated or getting upset, unless it's in direct response to a real and objective life trauma, suspect Reflexive Thinking. Ask this question: is what I'm upset about a *fact* (something that actually exists, an argument, loss of a job, an illness), or is it a *fiction* (something that could or might go wrong in the future)? Tell yourself, "I'm only allowed to be upset over facts." It's your choice: you can blindly accept insecurity's powerful hold (reacting to fiction) or learn to go forward (reacting only to facts). And if you decide to create the life you want, the better you understand the facts and truth of your life, the easier it will be to liberate yourself from the fictions.

❖ ❖ ❖

Self-Coaching Reflection
In any confrontation, being curious, rational, and looking
for the control connection can prevent you from mind-
lessly falling prey to Reflexive Thinking.

There are three reasons why Reflexive Thinking typically goes unchallenged:

1. It has become an automatic thinking habit that is part of your controlling juggle.

2. You're unaware that control is ruining and ruling your life, so Reflexive Thinking seems necessary and protective.

3. You don't have enough self-trust to reject the fictions of insecurity, or to risk trusting the facts and truth of your life.

Your Choice: Fact or Fiction

In anticipation of the five steps you will be taking shortly to reclaim your life, I'd like to give you a taste of what's ahead. You can begin right now to build a simple foundation of readiness by challenging some of your typical reflexes. Just referring to these heretofore unnoticed thoughts as Reflexive Thinking has the power to separate what's healthy and mature in you from what's defensive and destructive. You do this simply by asking yourself one question: "Is what I'm feeling fact or fiction?" This simple question has the power of disrupting insecurity's entire clandestine operation. Why? Because you're introducing consciousness to the situation. Remember, Reflexive Thinking has become automatic. It can run—and ruin—your life quite efficiently, especially if you're looking the other way! By just noticing the choice inherent in every struggle, you're exposing Reflexive Thinking. Once you see that you have choices, it's like that World War I–vintage song, "How Ya Gonna Keep 'Em Down on the Farm after They've Seen Paree?" Once you've seen the truth, the facts of your life, it's hard to go back to blindly accepting fiction.

Look at how easy this can be:

Reflexive Thinking	Truth Facts
I'm too old to go back to school.	Okay, I'll admit it, I'm afraid I might fail if I go back to school, but I don't have to let fear dictate my choice.
I can't socialize with them; I might embarrass myself.	That's my old reflex saying I can't socialize. When I'm relaxed, I know I do quite well.

I don't have a choice; I can't tell her no.	Of course I have a choice. It's only my reflex of doubt saying I can't say no.
Why did I say that? I'm such a jerk!	I'm allowed to mess up. It's just my reflex that says I have to be perfect.
I'll never amount to anything in life.	My habit is to throw in the towel, but I don't have to listen to that nonsense!
Sure I'm depressed; nothing ever works out for me.	There goes my knee-jerk whining again. With that attitude, nothing ever will work out for me! I don't have to agree with a doom-and-gloom view of the world.
You're asking me to call her? I can't do that. I can't handle confrontations.	It's not that I can't handle confrontations, it's that I'm afraid to risk handling them. If I go on avoiding every challenge, I'll never grow stronger. It's time to decide who I really want to be!
I'd like to be more secure, but it's just not me. It's not natural.	Insecurity may *feel* natural, but I know it's just a habit, not a reality. Sure it will probably feel unnatural at first, but so what? I deserve a better life, and I'm going to do what's necessary to get it.

Healthy Thinking

For now we can simply say that Healthy Thinking starts when Reflexive Thinking stops. Healthy, liberated, truth-based thinking is the antidote and is the goal of Self-Coaching. But for many people caught up in the throes of insecurity, Healthy Thinking remains only a remote possibility. What exactly is Healthy Thinking? Healthy Thinking is conscious problem-solving without the contamination of insecurity. Healthy Thinking also promotes a capacity for more spontaneous living highlighted by clarity of mind. But one thing Healthy Thinking will not do is eliminate all stress and anxiety from your life. In everyone's life there will always be challenges, obstacles, and pain, and this is normal. It's only when insecurity gets combined with a legitimate challenge that life becomes unwieldy.

Eileen, a thirty-four-year-old lawyer, learned about Healthy Thinking—the hard way.

When I first met Eileen her license to practice law had been suspended and she was about to be sued for legal malpractice. After the long-awaited trial date was announced, Eileen began to fall prey to depression, fits of rage, and devastating panic attacks. Her condition began to deteriorate rapidly as the trial began.

As her conditioned worsened, Eileen realized that any further decline would jeopardize her ability to function. Reflexive Thinking had taken a bad and tragic situation and turned it into an impossible nightmare. When called to testify, she found that not only couldn't she think clearly, but also she wound up becoming hysterical, requiring the judge to grant one of many recesses.

Her anxiety began to spill over into her life. She couldn't sleep, couldn't eat, and couldn't stop imagining that her husband (who was devoted and loving) would leave her, her kids would be shamed, and she would wind up in a mental hospital. As devastating as her legal situation was, it wasn't as devastating as her Reflexive Thinking led her to believe. Eileen was being swallowed up in worry and rumination and knew she was in trouble. That's when she called me.

From our first session, I realized the urgency in getting Eileen to separate herself from the stranglehold of Reflexive Thinking and begin to lay a foundation for some healthier thinking. I gave Eileen a crash course in Self-Talk, and together we charted a course for her to follow. She began by doing nothing more than insisting on not feeding her reflexive, runaway-train thoughts. She knew she couldn't afford to be casual about her efforts, and she wasn't. She battled her Reflexive Thinking like a warrior. Slowly she began to separate fact from fiction and refused to passively allow her insecurity to drive her down. As she began to make headway, she began to develop a resiliency and determination that both surprised and delighted her. No longer feeling distraught and victimized, she began to fight back with a tenacity and courage that began to have results.

Eileen had to work hard to maintain her healthy perspective, but once she put the brakes to Reflexive Thinking, her survival instincts were able to surface and carry the load for her. Healthy Thinking began to replace hysterical reflexes as her concentration, clarity, and effectiveness on the stand improved dramatically. She began getting more sleep and started to gain a resiliency that carried her through the trial. The case was eventually dismissed, her license was reinstated, and Eileen's family remained where they always had been, solidly behind her.

Whether it is a major crisis or a minor conflict, being able to step apart from Reflexive Thinking is the surest way to harness not only your capacity for Healthy Thinking, but also to tap into your reservoir of instinctual, intuitive energy and use it to ensure success.

Throwing the Switch

I've defined Reflexive Thinking as insecurity-driven, habit thinking. As everyone knows, habits have a tenacious capacity for resisting change. Mark Twain once quipped, "Smoking is the easiest habit in the world to break. I've done it thousands of times." Slippery or not, don't be fooled; the truth is, all habits are learned and all habits can be broken. I find that it helps to think of challenges as psychological light switches. Everyone has a switch. Flip the switch down and you unravel as insecurity dictates the course of your life. Flip it up and you choose to handle life instead of letting it deplete you. What determines which way you throw the switch? It's your ability to risk trusting truth rather than fiction.

In the chapters that follow, Self-Coaching will ensure that you throw the switch up. But for now, just understand that turning your life around isn't going to be as hard as you may think—not once you stop listening to Reflexive Thinking telling you it's impossible.

Which way are you going to throw that switch? When rocked by life, are you going to continue to listen to Reflexive Thinking, or are you going to risk finding the truth?

Tammy, a twenty-six-year-old mother of two, was plagued with guilt over thoughts that she was an inadequate mother. Nothing she did ever seemed to be enough. She feared that her inadequacy would one day wind up causing her to lose custody of her children. It didn't matter that her husband and children thought she was fantastic! It didn't matter because her Reflexive Thinking had been tossing her emotions around like a rag doll. Tammy was depleted and had no question that she needed to throw the switch, but she was afraid:

> How can I possibly trust me when there's a part of me creating so much fear? How do I choose not to believe the fears? To feel I'm really okay? How do I choose to get on with my life and truly know these thoughts are all bull and that I'm not hurting my kids? I feel like I'm being trampled by my insecurities. They feel so strong, and I don't know what to do. No, I'm not being honest. It's not entirely true that I don't know what to do; I do know. The truth is I just can't seem to do it. It's as if I feel powerless to stop this broken record, even though I know that is exactly what I must do. How do I convince myself that these thoughts are just fictions? If it had to do with anything other than my kids, I wouldn't have to be so uptight. I can't afford to take a risk with their well-being.

I responded:

> When you were young, did you believe in the bogeyman? If you did, then you may remember how much you suffered at the hands

of your imagination. In a sense, what's happening now is that your insecurity has created a bogeyman reflex—a fiction of fear that you're a terrible mother, and you're allowing yourself to believe it. You're the victim of Reflexive Thinking that insists you can't trust your perceptions. Rather than knee-jerk hysterics, you must try to see the truth! Force yourself to see life as it is, not as your insecurity paints it. The solution is no different now than when you were a child: you must turn on the light once again— the light of consciousness. Then only the truth will remain—no bogeyman.

Now, fortified with an understanding of Reflexive Thinking and a bit of practice, you'll be amazed at how obvious and easy it becomes to detect whether it's you who's really doing your thinking or insecurity that's thinking for you. By detecting the influence of Reflexive Thinking, you'll be able to eliminate all bogeymen from your life. You'll also be able to risk believing truth over fiction. Do this, and your life will begin to soar. In fact, you won't be able to prevent it.

7

Stop Insulating
and Avoiding

When your Reflexive Thinking has you convinced that you're no match for life, insulating and avoiding life's challenges is a common, yet misguided, defense. This defense is an attempt to insulate yourself from harm's way. Just as a winter coat insulates you from the cold, the controlling strategy of insulation attempts to create a protective buffer zone, a barrier between you and perceived danger. Some very routine, everyday experiences can become forms of psychological insulation when driven by insecurity. It's an extensive list that can include emotional detachment (coldness), excessive reading or watching TV, alcohol or substance abuse, passivity, workaholism, anger or hostility, social avoidance or shyness, aloofness, excessive fatigue or sleep, depression, even gaining weight. Although any of these expressions, when excessive, may be cause for concern, they are rarely seen for what they are—controlling strategies that insulate and excuse you from life.

Since an insulated life is rarely seen as a major contributor to your unhappiness or lack of success, it's important to use the following self-quiz to help you assess whether you've been trying to gain control over your life by avoiding it.

The Defense of Insulation Self-Quiz

Please read the following questions carefully, but don't overthink your responses. Circle your responses as being either mostly true or mostly false as they generally pertain to your life. Answer each question even if you're not completely sure. Scoring is at the end of the test.

T F I usually feel most comfortable when I'm alone or with family.

T F I have no problem entertaining myself.

T F Although I may not show it, I'm usually guarded around people.

T F I don't like it when someone does me a favor (I'd rather give than receive).

T F I don't have many close friends.

T F I tend to enjoy solitary activities or hobbies.

T F I have a tendency to overindulge in alcohol or drugs.

T F I like most forms of escape (e.g., projects, work, TV, video games, reading).

T F I'd rather clean a closet (busywork) than go out with friends.

T F People often wind up disappointing me.

T F I'm shy.

T F Depending on my mood, I often screen my phone calls.

T F I'm not very spontaneous.

T F I've been criticized for being emotionally aloof or detached.

T F I have a tendency to become hostile when I feel defensive.

T F I tend to keep my real feelings hidden from others.

T F I seem to have trouble with emotional intimacy.

T F My temper has gotten me into trouble.

T F I tell a lot of white lies.

T F Relationships are mostly problems.

If you scored more than 14 "true," you have definite insulating tendencies and need to recognize the importance of not letting these particular habits persist without some Self-Coaching intervention. A score of 9 to 14 suggests a moderate tendency toward insulation. Be aware of the warnings in this chapter, and don't allow any progression toward insulation or escapism to develop. A score of less than 9 indicates few significant insulating tendencies. You may, however, be prone to occasional insulating strategies when dealing with stress.

Unhealthy Insulation, Healthy Insulation

Insulating yourself from danger may sound like a good idea—and it is—as long as you remember a distinction we made in chapter 4 between thinking that is circumstance-driven (the good kind) and thinking that is insecurity-driven (the bad kind). Trying to separate healthy (good) from unhealthy (bad) insulation can be a bit challenging at first because of the subtle differences between the two. As you read through the following examples, see if you can recognize how, when driven by circumstances (facts), insulation tends to be more rational, proportionate, and tempered. When driven by insecurity (fictions), on the other hand, notice how the responses tend to be highly reactive, impulsive, and disproportionate to the situation at hand. Also note how healthy insulation is driven *only* by facts. Unhealthy insulation may start out as a reaction to facts but sooner or later begins to turn those facts into fictions:

Circumstance-driven insulation: I just learned that my colleague is bad-mouthing me to the boss [fact]. I'm going to watch what I say for a while.

Insecurity-driven insulation: My boss wasn't very pleasant with me this morning [fact]. Someone must be bad-mouthing me [fiction]. From now on, I'm not going to talk to anyone!

Circumstance-driven insulation: Bob is so competitive he actually told me he's going to have my job in six months [fact]! Unfortunately, I'm going to have to protect myself and make sure all my files are up to date.

Insecurity-driven insulation: Bob seems like a dangerous guy [fact]. I bet he's trying to undermine me to the boss [fiction]. I don't need this stress. I'm going to quit! Who needs this job, anyway?

Circumstance-driven insulation: My old boyfriend is going to be at the party [fact]. I certainly have no intention of talking to him.

Insecurity-driven insulation: What? My old boyfriend is going to be at the party [fact]? With all this weight I've gained I'm sure he would be repulsed if he saw me [fiction]. No, I'm not going to the party.

Circumstance-driven insulation: Sherry is too opinionated [fact]. I find it a lot less stressful to let her make the decisions whenever we're together.

Insecurity-driven insulation: Sherry wants to join us tonight [fact]? I think I'm just going to stay home tonight. All of a sudden, I'm feeling too tired to go out. Anyway, no one really cares if I join them [fiction].

Circumstance-driven insulation: My mother calls me constantly [fact]. She's driving me crazy [fact]. From now on I'm going to get a phone answering machine and begin to screen some of her calls.

Insecurity-driven insulation: I don't think I have a choice [fiction]; I'm just going to give my mother the cold shoulder. Sooner or later she'll get the hint and stop calling.

Circumstance-driven insulation: Cathy always winds up annoying me [fact]. There's no reason I need to see her so often.

Insecurity-driven insulation: I couldn't possibly let Cathy down; it would kill her [fiction]. From now on, when Cathy and I go out, I'm going to insist we go to a club. Once I have a few glasses of wine I should be okay.

Let me summarize the essential differences between unhealthy and healthy insulation:

Unhealthy Insulation

Because of insecurity (not circumstance), you insulate yourself from life to feel more in control. (Fictions are treated as facts.)

For example: avoiding a conversation because you're afraid you might say something you'll regret; not buying a snowblower because you're afraid your neighbors may expect you to remove their snow; not going to the company picnic because you don't want to take a chance that you might drink too much; avoiding intimacy because you feel you'll expose too much of yourself.

Insulation is unhealthy when it becomes disproportionate to the circumstance.

For example: refusing to see a doctor because you don't want to be told you have to lose weight; selling your house because you've found a mouse; breaking up with your boyfriend because you found him looking at another girl; refusing to ever fly again because of terrorism.

Healthy Insulation

Insulation is healthy when you're avoiding a legitimate, threatening life circumstance (fact) to protect yourself or to provide necessary psychological or physical restoration. Protecting yourself from all forms of danger is healthy.

For example: telling your tennis partner that you need to take a break from the competition; keeping a safe distance from someone who's got the flu; declining an invitation because you're too tired; getting a sitter and making weekend reservations at a bed-and-breakfast because of an ongoing struggle with your kids; putting down your work and going out for a walk.

It's okay to insulate yourself from a legitimate threat or challenge that you're not prepared for.

For example: postponing a test that you weren't able to study for; not wanting to go on a blind date without first getting more information; not running in a marathon until you've discussed it with your doctor; avoiding intimacy until you feel more comfortable with someone.

Insulation is reasonable when it's proportionate and appropriate to the circumstance.

For example: not wanting to be around someone who is obnoxious; not wanting to continue dating someone who has cheated on you; not wanting to drive after having a few drinks; avoiding people whom you feel incompatible with; not feeling guilty for not returning your mother's call after you've spoken with her three times in the past three hours.

Since healthy forms of insulation are always a plus, we can now abandon any further discussion of them and focus our full attention on the bad, insecurity-driven expressions of insulation. For the sake of brevity, from this point on I will refer to insecurity-driven insulation simply as insulation.

Shell Living

What do clams, oysters, lobsters, turtles, and armadillos have in common? They all rely on their shells for protection from the world. When confronted with a life challenge, insulation can provide you with a formidable shell. Maybe a psychological shell isn't as hard as an oyster or armadillo shell, but make no mistake: when it comes to feeling in control, it can be just as impenetrable.

Most things psychological can be expressed very clearly if you think of a balance scale. What you take away from one side, you give to the other. As one tendency grows, its opposite weakens. Keep building your shell of insulation and you invariably wind up weakening your muscles to handle life. It's really that straightforward.

Charlie, a forty-year-old physical education teacher at a local high school, had been "avoiding and insulating" for nineteen years when he came to see me. And although he didn't realize it at the time, he was primed and ready to risk poking his head out of his shell and engaging life. According to Charlie:

> I get home exhausted every night and the last thing I want to do
> is talk to anyone on the phone. I usually turn off the ringer and
> let the answering machine pick up. After a few days I begin to feel
> guilty, especially when my mother keeps calling, saying, "I never

know if you're alive or dead." I really don't get it. Why can't people accept the fact that I'd rather be left alone? They don't want to understand that.

My evenings have become a lonely ritual of watching TV, poking around on the Internet, and drinking beer. Don't get me wrong, I'm not drinking to get drunk, it's just something to do. And now look at me: I haven't been to the gym in more than a year, and my gut has been getting way out of control. What I should be doing is going out and trying to meet some girls, but now . . . look at me, I'm a tank! I can't win.

Everything and everyone seem like a burden. I know I keep saying it, but I just want to be left alone. Funny, if I'm honest, when I'm alone pounding down the beers, I'm not happy. In fact, I'd say I'm depressed. Not suicidal or anything, just feeling sorry for myself. And the more down I feel, the more impossible it is for me to want to be around anyone else. That's why I decided to try some counseling. Maybe I need to accept the fact that I'm a loner. Maybe I need to accept the fact that it's just the way it is, right?

Not quite, Charlie; that's not the way it "is," it's just the way it feels! Charlie's been fertilizing a long-standing insecurity about the old if-only-I-had-gone-left-instead-of-right malaise. When he was in college, Charlie began using marijuana regularly. He had been determined to major in chemistry and then go to medical school. After all, he was the apple of his parents' eye who could do no wrong. Since he was a child, everyone expected Charlie to be a star. In fact, his mother, in an attempt to be both cute and informative, would introduce him by saying, "This is my son, Dr. Charlie."

Then, in his sophomore year of college, came the drugs and the partying. As his grades began to slide, Charlie found the demands of organic chemistry and maintaining straight A's too much to handle. Without much thought, he shifted his major to education, which he found to be both manageable and less demanding than premed.

Charlie managed to get away from drugs and eventually graduated.

The school where he did his student teaching had an opening, and Charlie began work immediately. For the past nineteen years Charlie's been harboring an attitude of self-deprecation: "I have to admit it, when I meet a girl, I'm embarrassed to tell her what I do. Once or twice, I did lie and say I was a surgeon. That wasn't very smart, but I just had to feel what it was like."

As Charlie and I began to explore his insulated lifestyle, we were able to identify the following insulating traits:

1. Insulated thinking: name-calling, self-defeating negatives, and put-downs ("I need to accept the fact that I'm a loser" or "I'm a second-class citizen")

2. Insulated avoidance: turning off the phone

3. Insulated avoidance: refusing to socialize

4. Insulated avoidance: isolating himself in his office

5. Insulated hostility: feeling angry and hostile as means of creating distance

6. Insulated depressed mood: rationale for pulling away (low energy, feeling overwhelmed, not caring, feeling sorry for himself)

7. Insulated avoidance: drinking

Using Self-Coaching, Charlie began to challenge his prejudices by learning to look for the truth rather than blindly sitting back and allowing Reflexive Thinking to spin out fictions of remorse and regret. He enjoyed what he did and was damn good at it, but his Reflexive Thinking made it impossible for him to appreciate this simple reality. Charlie once told me, after a particularly good day at school, that he felt almost guilty about enjoying himself! Why guilty? Because, up until now, if he enjoyed being a teacher, his insecurity told him he was letting his parents down.

Here's the amazing part of all this. Within months after Charlie's transformation from self-loathing insulation to a recognition of his special gifts and loves, he met a woman to whom he is currently engaged. Call it what you want—coincidence, serendipity—the fact remains: as Charlie's attitude shifted, so did his luck. The chicken or the egg? I've seen this type of "coincidence" too many times to ignore it. Negativity seems to breed negative results, while positivity seems to breed success. In a later chapter I'm going to address how your thoughts and beliefs can actually alter your destiny and your luck. I know one has nothing to do with the other (at least not causally), but somehow, what we believe—*really* believe—seems to affect our destiny.

Happiness Is Looking for You

There's a German proverb, *Begin to weave, and God will give you the thread.* Begin to believe in yourself; the answers will find you. I believe this philosophy wholeheartedly and use it all the time when I counsel people. If you trust that answers can and will find you, it begins to lessen the reliance on your ego-driven need to figure it all out. It's all your figuring that's bogged you down in the first place. For the control person, when it comes to discovering how to be happy, less is more.

You may feel it's a bit reckless to try to downgrade your thoughts by adopting a more open and expansive receptivity to life—after all, until now, controlling life (vis-à-vis thoughts) seemed to be your only true friend. But the truth remains that your way hasn't been working! Straining, struggling, and trying to control life haven't produced the answers you've hoped for. Quite the contrary; they've only produced more problems.

I need to challenge you to abandon any shell that represents your Reflexive Thinking approach to handling life and begin to recognize that there's more to you than your thoughts tell you. Answers, happiness, meaning, and purpose can find you only if you replace congested, clogged, control thinking with a willingness to believe in that vast instinctual ocean that is your *other potential.*

Self-Coaching Reflection

I find that the harder I work, the more luck I seem to have.

—Thomas Jefferson

115

Emotionally Cold People

There's another form of shell insulation that's characterized by retracting into a shell of emotional avoidance. Problems that fall into this category include fear of commitment or intimacy, emotional restriction or suppression, and shyness or aloofness. Why is life without emotion a defense of insulation? Because emotions are less controllable than thoughts, and if you're not careful, you can wind up exposing more than you can handle. Whereas thoughts can be more readily controlled, emotions divulge the raw truth about what's really going on within you. It's a toothpaste-out-of-the-tube experience that can be intimidating for someone struggling to control life. And for this type of person, sidestepping emotions can be just the ticket for controlling exactly what you want people to see.

Cynthia's account of her emotionally insulated husband will provide a glimpse of this rather subtle yet potentially devastating form of control:

> I love Mark, but sometimes I question his love for me. Although he says he loves me, he never shows it. He'll talk about anything, even our relationship, but he never shows any feelings. When I try to pin him down and ask him how he feels about something, I keep getting the same "I don't know" response. Mark's not cold, it's just that there's no . . . expression.
>
> Come to think of it, I guess Mark does show some emotion. Occasionally he'll lose his temper, but that's about the only emotion I ever see. Usually he's just flat, bland, middle-of-the-road Mark. Even our lovemaking is like this. It's more mechanical and routine. Sometimes I wonder why I'm not turned off. There's no warmth or affection, and God forbid I suggest we do anything a bit more adventurous. Mark is definitely not a risk taker. When we're intimate he needs the lights out, no talk or foreplay . . . it's almost like he's just trying to get through the experience.
>
> Mark doesn't relate to anyone. Guess that's just who he is. Even

with the kids, I find him fidgeting and squirming when they want to cuddle or give him a kiss. It's like he's scared to death of something. Lord only knows what it might be. I sure don't.

Cynthia and Mark began couples counseling, and both were quite receptive to the notion that there really was another Mark—one hidden and cloistered away in his shell of avoidance. It took a bit of coaching to get Mark to risk exposing feelings, but once he did, things began to change rapidly.

Cynthia's instincts were correct all along: Mark wasn't a cold person at all. In fact, he was a very sensitive, warm, and loving person who had long ago begun a habit that insisted his feelings were too intense and dangerous. Mark vividly recalled his macho, ironworker father's motto: *Boys have to be men.* While growing up, exposing feelings—any feelings—brought on a reflexive anxiety reminiscent of the many times he was ridiculed for being a "mama's boy." At an early age Mark figured out that holding back his emotions was by far the safer strategy. Mark began a personality transformation from sensitivity to stoicism. The only thing that mattered was that he wasn't taunted about being a "mama's boy." In those formative years, Mark forged a primitive form of insulation that had now become his lifelong habit. And only now was he beginning to challenge it. Thanks to Cynthia.

When I asked Mark to challenge his perception that emotions were too dangerous, he was unable to give one rational reason why they were dangerous. All he could say was, "They're dangerous because they just feel dangerous." Mark needed to learn some Self-Coaching: *when Reflexive Thinking is steering, the thoughts you have and the feelings you feel can't be trusted.* It's not that Mark was afraid of reality, he was afraid of a ghost fear that twisted his perceptions and held him hostage. And here's where a coaching approach rather than a traditional therapeutic approach really paid off.

Although we were interested in Mark's insulation history, as intriguing as it was to try to pin down the origins of his habit, I need to remind you once again that Self-Coaching doesn't require you to revisit the past. Since all habits are expressed and reflected in the present, why waste time in the past? Instead of insights or laborious historical explorations, Mark needed to be challenged, motivated, and convinced that he could break the bonds of insecurity that were irrationally controlling his life in the present.

Self-Coaching Reflection
If at halftime, a basketball coach had his players explore the historical underpinnings of why they were losing, chances are there would be five confused players on that court going into the second half. A good coach needs to do three things: decide what needs to be done, light a fire of motivation, and get his team to do it—now!

Once Mark had a foundation of understanding and truth to work from, he began to experiment. At first his emotions were only wisps of feelings, subtle and almost overlooked, but the more he risked, the more he became aware of a whole new world of experience. Without emotional insulation, Mark was allowing *it* to find *him*. As Cynthia put it in one of our last sessions, "I've always loved Mark, but now I can finally see why. Now I can see a whole person."

Anger Management

> *Whatever is begun in anger ends in shame.*
>
> —Benjamin Franklin

There's one last expression of insulation: using anger as a way of insulating yourself from life. These are life's growlers. They're people who can be perfectly amiable as long as you're not ruffling their feathers. But watch out if you do! They'll growl, bark, snarl, and maybe even bite your head off. Since anger and rage seem to be states of uncontrollable emotion, it's probably not obvious why these are attempts to control through insulation. The answer is straightforward: *If you threaten me and I become hostile, then I can intimidate you and push you away. And the farther away from me I push you, the more insulated I feel.*

Let me give my usual disclaimer at this point: I'm talking about insecurity-driven hostility, not circumstance-driven. It's not inappropriate or unhealthy to get angry when you slam your finger with a hammer (circumstance-driven). Nor is it unhealthy to let someone know how you feel when he or she intentionally tries to hurt you. Anger, when appropriate to the circumstance, can be a way of mobilizing energy and confidence. But when anger is *inappropriate* to the circumstance (a fiction), then we're dealing with insecurity. It would be unhealthy, for example, to turn on your wife and embarrass her in front of company because she mentioned that you didn't get your promotion: "I may not have gotten my promotion, but look who's talking! The only promotion you ever got was because the boss has the hots for you!" Ouch!

Obviously in the above example, this guy's going to wind up with a lot more chaos because of his hostile remarks than had he said nothing. But if you're a growler, your modus operandi is to reflexively *attack and distance*. Pushing someone away makes you feel insulated, at least for the moment. It's a "who needs 'em?" attitude that, when habituated, can become one of the most damaging and dangerous of all the control strategies.

Maybe you've found yourself embarrassed by your outbursts, your screaming like a lunatic in the car if someone cuts you off, or your totally out-of-proportion impatience with the salesclerk at the supermarket. If hostility or rage have become a fixture in your life, then you must understand that in those critical seconds before emotionally throwing yourself to the lions, you do have a choice. Like all habits of insecurity, anger is no different. Feed it, fertilize it, and it will grow. But with hostility there's only a narrow window of opportunity for you to employ some effective Self-Coaching. Miss that opportunity, begin sliding down anger's slippery slope, and it's too late. Anger will take over and deposit you wherever it damn well chooses.

This brings us to a very important point. Whether it is anger, hostility, anxiety, depression, or panic, Reflexive Thinking has a cumulative effect on your life. Although most problems are preceded by "seed" thoughts, sometimes these thoughts are imperceptible. With certain problems, particularly hostility, you'll seemingly go from light to dark in a split second. If this is the case for you, it's important to understand that control living accumulates friction, leaving you vulnerable and susceptible to a crash.

If you find it hard to pick up the "seed" thoughts that precede any kind of a meltdown, you'll be using Self-Coaching to become more aggressive with your ongoing, daily skirmishes, attempting to starve your insecurity before it reaches a point where your natural resilience has been depleted. Because once depleted, you're left with a hair-trigger emotionality that will often leave you primed and ready for an explosion.

Mindfulness

If you've noticed you're losing your temper more easily; if anger, rage, hostility, or violence have begun to erupt in your life; or if you've become enamored with living a shell type of life, it's time to cultivate an attitude of mindfulness. Mindfulness might best be described as a kind of ongoing directed awareness of your motions and emotions. Rather than being a bystander, passively watching your life unfold, mindfulness puts you at the active center of your life. As you continue to learn and understand the true nature of struggle (control, habit, insecurity), you'll find that you can begin to pay a more focused attention to what's happening in your life. Your life is no longer pure reflex; now you're beginning to separate healthy from unhealthy, fact from fiction, all prerequisites to Self-Coaching's five steps that you'll be using to create the life you want.

So many people I've worked with are confused about this seemingly "spontaneous" or "instantaneous" quality to anger as well as other forms of insulated control. Granted, it may *feel* like you are blindsided by anger, fear, or a need to defend, but now you know that you can't always trust what you feel, especially when your feelings are driven by insecurity. Once you get used to mindfully being part of your process of change, you'll begin to see that more often than not, there will be certain trigger thoughts. Things do happen quickly when your temperature is rising, but not so quickly that you don't have a choice. There's *always* a choice. You need to learn to see it.

When you pull a trigger on a gun, the cartridge explodes. Similarly, a trigger thought can ignite a reflexive response of fight, flight, or freeze. Since emotions can flare up quickly (once caught up in the emotional moment, it's almost impossible to reverse things), it's important for you to recognize that the window of opportunity is small—you must take immediate action. Since many forms of control are served by impulsive reacting, especially anger and hostility, a kind of mindless compliance, *refuse to comply!* By cultivating a mindful attitude you can begin the process of taking your life back. Every challenge—whether it's being told no to a request, a disagreement with your husband, someone cutting you off on the road, or vague fears of danger or threat—is an opportunity for you to say no to insecurity and to insist *I have a choice!* All your efforts will have a cumulative effect. There are no insignificant or small battles; every effort is part of a muscle-building campaign. Anger, rage, and all kinds of shell living are habits, just like any other habit. So what are you waiting for? *Stop* feeding them!

Self-Coaching Reflection
Anger and rage are habits that will own you . . .
if you permit them to.

8

A Perfect Way to Be Miserable

When your hobbies get in the way of your work, that's okay; but
when your hobbies get in the way of themselves . . . well . . .

—Steve Martin

When I was eleven, my parents bought me a model ship for my birthday. This was no ordinary model. For months I had perched myself outside the five-and-ten store hoping that the three-masted schooner would still be available when my birthday rolled around. It was! When the big day arrived, I couldn't open the box fast enough. Lifting the lid and peering at the treasure within, I was ecstatic. I had never seen anything quite like it. It was enormous, more than three feet long from bow sprit to stern. The detail of each piece was so exact you could see the wood grain in the decking. The rigging on the sails actually had working, threaded pulleys, and there was even a crew, clothed in bandannas and knickers. I was speechless.

I started out in earnest, minutes quickly turning to hours, morning to night. My mother eventually admonished me: "If you don't put that down and go to bed, I'll never buy you another model." What? She wanted me to put it down? To stop? I could no more stop building that model than I could stop breathing. She didn't—couldn't—understand. Truth was, I couldn't completely understand the force, the compulsion, that was driving me that day. I didn't feel I had a choice, I *had* to finish building the model. What started out as euphoria had turned into a growing pressure. I felt possessed.

Somewhere in my frenzy to complete the model, I vaguely recall reading a warning: "Some applications require thorough drying before continuing." If I waited for the glue to dry I'd never finish! I had to risk ignoring the warning. After all, I was just beginning to make headway—I needed to finish before my mother returned to my room and started yelling.

Then it happened. The mainmast (whose glue had not dried), laboring under the weight of the rigging, began to list, then fall. Quickly, frantically, I applied more glue. Then more. I had to stop this catastrophe. The glue wasn't working! Uneasiness quickly turned into panic as I tried to secure the mast, first by tying it with thread to anything that would serve as an anchor. This was not working, so I grabbed two encyclopedias from the shelf and sandwiched the mast between them—it held! I managed to save my ship. I began to breathe. Relieved.

Even at eleven years old, I knew I had gone too far. I had pushed fate and almost got what I deserved. I knew, and was grateful, that I had dodged the bullet. Or so I thought. That's when I saw it. In my haste, I had inadvertently dropped a glob of glue on the beautiful, wood-simulated deck! I quickly tried to wipe it away with my finger—it smudged! I tried again desperately. More smudge. Damp cloth, alcohol, nail polish remover—worse. Much worse! The drop of glue had grown grotesque, disfiguring and ruining my beautiful ship.

For a long moment I sat transfixed, emotionless, frozen in a prelude to despair. Slowly the realization that my model was ruined began to reach my consciousness. I wanted to cry, scream; mostly I wanted to explode. The tension I felt was unbearable. I hated that model! I wanted to throw it against the wall, to hurt it for what it did to me. It didn't help when my mother came in saying, "See, I told you to leave it until morning!" Of course she was right, I knew it, but I didn't have a choice. At that point I lost it. I was inconsolable.

The next day my mother asked me about the model. She wanted to know why I wasn't going to finish it. I remember staring at her blankly. "Finish it? You must be kidding! It's ruined!" She couldn't understand that for me the model had died. The glue smudge was a knife through the heart of the project. It was no longer a thing of ecstasy, it was now only a deformed, amorphous lump of plastic. With a smudge.

To my mother's disbelief, I wound up throwing the model away. It was all I could do.

Me, a Perfectionist?

There are many reasons why your life may falter, but none so misguided as striving for perfection. Perhaps you never considered yourself a diehard perfectionist; if so, you may be surprised to learn that perfectionism isn't just for perfectionists. Nor is it just for those who demand excellence as the royal road to security and happiness. Perfectionistic habits can infiltrate your life in various and subtle forms of compulsion, obsession, or rigidity. Whether you're afraid of saying the wrong thing, unable to say no, feeling conspicuous about the stain on your blouse, obsessive about your weight, or just have to run that one extra mile, the desire to get beyond criticism by eliminating life's flaws is one of insecurity's most demanding lifestyles.

In spite of the demands perfection striving puts on your life, you've probably never questioned your lofty goals. After all, bosses, teachers, and friends all seem to applaud your efforts and successes. Right? You rarely get into trouble or wind up being criticized, so what's wrong with wanting to be perfect? Nothing—that is, if it were obtainable, if it were manageable, and if it wasn't ruining your life! But, rather than prejudice you, let's start out with a self-quiz. You might be surprised by the results.

Perfectionism Self-Quiz

Please read the following questions carefully, but don't overthink your responses. Circle your responses as being either mostly true or mostly false as they generally pertain to your life. Answer each question even if you're not completely sure. Scoring is at the end of the test.

T   F   My appearance matters too much.

T   F   I'm too critical.

T	F	I tend to be a black-and-white thinker.
T	F	I don't handle physical ailments very well.
T	F	I would say I'm compulsive.
T	F	I'm more driven than relaxed.
T	F	I'm always feeling I "should" or "have to" do something.
T	F	I usually don't feel I have a choice in life.
T	F	I often feel tension or anxiety.
T	F	I'm not very flexible.
T	F	I get too upset when things go wrong.
T	F	When I look in a mirror, I always find fault.
T	F	I'm too fat (too thin).
T	F	I'm a worrier.
T	F	My goals are much more important than the process involved in reaching them.
T	F	I fuss too much when I'm getting ready.
T	F	I can't leave something that's out of place.
T	F	If you want to get a job done right, you have to do it yourself.
T	F	I'm rarely caught off guard.
T	F	I've been accused of being too neat (or fanatical, or obsessive).
T	F	I've been told I'm too rigid.
T	F	I seem to be more intellectual than emotional.
T	F	If you can't do something 100 percent, don't do it.
T	F	Whatever I do, it has to be done just so, or I can't put it down.
T	F	I tend to overdo everything.

A score of 1 to 8 "true" answers indicates a mild normal degree of perfectionism. You'll be using this book more for personality expansion rather than for repair.

A score of 9 to 17 "true" answers indicates a moderate level of perfectionism. Your compulsive demands are probably undermining your capacity for effective and successful living. You can expect this book to change significantly your view and experience of the world without jeopardizing your success.

If you scored 18 or more "true" answers, your self-worth and confidence have been eroded by perfectionistic demands. You'll need to restructure your thoughts and perceptions to establish more adequate self-trust. You can expect that your gains will have a major, positive impact on your life as well as on your overall happiness.

Trying Less and Feeling More

Let's go back to my shipbuilding experience mentioned at the beginning of this chapter. I know now that it wasn't just about building a model, it was a crusade to build the *perfect* model. Actually, I never decided—at least not consciously—that it had to be perfect, that was just the way I approached life back then. Reflexively. The drive toward perfection is a kind of possession, not by a curse or a devil, but by Reflexive Thinking that demands flawlessness. My possession that day had two components: build the perfect model and build it *now!* But what exactly was my hurry?

To answer this question, you'll need to know a few additional facts about my life. For me, even at age eleven, I was already well on my way to becoming a control hound. Insecurity had long ago sent roots of doubt and fear deep into my psyche, to which I responded with a reflexive juggle of various control strategies dominated by shoulds and have-tos. As an only child, I had become very sensitive to my mother's need for me to be her "perfect little boy." Without going too deeply into my history, let's just say that my perception was that if I did anything to upset her, she would die. Long before I understood what it meant, I had been told, "Your mother has a rheumatic heart; don't get her upset." The seeds of my insecurity had thus been sown at a young age. *I felt responsible for keeping my mother alive!* My task seemed straightforward: *I can't upset my mother, and I've got to be perfect.*

Now back to my model. Obviously, my need for perfection and control had gone beyond pleasing and protecting my mother (if you recall, I was willing to upset her rather than restrain my compulsive desire to finish). What started out as a mandate to keep my mother alive had now grown, by age eleven, into a compulsive way of life. It was now my habit. No longer was I *trying* to be perfect, now I didn't have a choice. I was the victim of a reflexive way of living—I *had* to be perfect. My experience that day with the model is a perfect snapshot of who I had become. The thought that someone might say, "Gee, Joey, your model is so nice . . . wait, what's that awful smudge?" was not something I felt I could handle. The model—and Joe Luciani—had to be beyond criticism. Why? Because this was the control my Reflexive Thinking demanded. And to be beyond criticism, one must be perfect.

The Illusion of Security

Helen Keller once said, "Security is mostly a superstition. It does not exist in nature." What I was seeking to accomplish by building the perfect model was indeed superstition—a myth, a fiction: *If I can build this model perfectly, it will give me security.* Security, like control, is an illusion. You'll never figure out how to own security, nor can you ever possess it once you feel it. If it were any other way, there would be a formula that could teach you to eliminate fear, psychological pain and suffering, even death from your life. Security is a relative term.

As mentioned in an earlier chapter, since no one grows up in a perfect world and no one has perfect parents, it's not whether you're secure or insecure, it's to what extent you are. At this point in my life, I can report to you that I am a *relatively* secure person. I would be lying if I omitted the qualifier "relatively" from my description. If I told you I was totally secure—and if I believed this—I would be declaring that I had a perfect life. Thank God I no longer chase that myth. I've learned that life doesn't have to be controlled, nor do I have to be perfect, to feel safe. It's not control that brings the feeling of security, it's trust.

How did my approach to life change from my days of chasing perfection? It's been a long evolution for me, and being a psychologist helps. Like a computer technician who's always upgrading the family computer, you bring home what you learn. Self-Coaching has been one of my "upgrades." I've come to accept that there will be occasional "smudges" in my life. And that's okay. I learn a lot from my smudges and I become a better person. In this context, smudges are an important part of my maturation. But most important, when I look at my life, I no longer look only at the errant drop of glue. Now I see the bigger picture.

Self-Coaching Reflection
Psychological maturity can be defined as a progression
from Reflexive Thinking to courageous living.

It's pure, unadulterated poppycock to think that there are smudgeless people in this world. What's equally absurd is the notion that you have no choice, that you have to be perfect: "I don't have the same luxury as everyone else; I have to be the best." If you believe that you're different from others—that you don't have a choice—you're being hoodwinked! It may *feel* as if you don't have a choice, but this isn't true. You do have a choice. You're just rolling over and surrendering to this feeling and the Reflexive Thinking that supports it. You're just Fido on a leash being tugged around by insecurity.

Self-Coaching Reflection
Perfectionism isn't about being perfect, it's about not
wanting to feel insecure.

Stars: Those Who Have to Shine

Sometimes this perception of having no choice can be cloaked in arrogance: "You can't expect *me* to go out looking like this. No way! I have an image to protect!" When, because of a habit of perfection, you've become identified with being a "Star," you might find it hard to imagine letting your fans down.

Self-Coaching Reflection
Perfectionism is the enemy of legitimate happiness
and serenity.

Every life has its flaws, blemishes, pimples, smudges, and errors. For a Star, these aren't simply annoyances or frustrations, they're cataclysmic events that can throw your life into chaos. Stars may tell you that they know they're being ridiculous, but knowing this doesn't stop them from canceling a date because of a zit or getting depressed because the boss forgot to say "great job" on the project. What about you? Do flaws diminish your life? Your worth? Do you need to be the center of attention, the lead in the play, or the proverbial teacher's pet?

Self-Coaching Reflection
Life truth 1: No one and no life is without flaw
or smudge.

A friend once told me, and I don't know if it's true, that during the Chinese Ming dynasty, the artisans who crafted those serenely beautiful ceramics would intentionally chip away a minute piece of the base to be released from having to seek perfection. Smart people. They knew that perfection is the enemy of creation. If you're trying too hard not to mess up, then your creative vitality, your serenity, and your effectiveness will all be held in check.

The Real Difference between Success and Failure

As a psychologist, I work hard at understanding why I do what I do, but I'm not unreasonable. I know I make mistakes. I don't always hit a bull's-eye. Over the years I've changed the way I see things. I no longer see my lack of perfection as me being flawed. As long as my intentions and effort are from the heart, I see my imperfections not as failures, but as challenges and opportunities to learn. And I no longer have to be the best—although this is nice when it happens. Now it's enough to know I *tried* my best and fought the good fight.

To me, failure means quitting. If, for example, I try to figure out why my VCR won't record a TV program and don't succeed, I refuse to see this as a failure. Who knows? Perhaps tomorrow I'll figure out that you first have to set the clock on the VCR before the timer will work. Then my initial lack of success wasn't a failure—it was a prelude to success! In life it's not the slope of the path or the impediments along the way that dictate success—it's your determination.

Self-Coaching Reflection
I have not failed. I've just found ten thousand ways
that won't work.

—Thomas Alva Edison

The truth that sets me free is the realization that to evolve and grow and mature, I need all my experiences—positive *and* negative. Sometimes, as with the example of my VCR, I find that after a period of frustrated trying and lack of success, an insight can leap into my mind. That's the old "ah-ha" experience. Elias Howe, the inventor of the sewing machine, was struggling for months with his idea. It was reported that he had a dream, where he recalled seeing natives in an African tribe standing in front of him, each with a spear pointing into the dirt. They began to rhythmically raise and lower their spears, all of which had curiously hollowed-out spear heads. He awoke with his inspiration to place the eye of the needle at the point and to thrust the thread through the fabric instead of drawing it after.

Prior to his insight, Mr. Howe could have thrown up his hands over his many months of frustration, declaring he was a failure. But he wasn't a failure; he just hadn't yet reached his success. I don't know about you, but I learned long ago that lack of success can be much more instructive than success. A perception of failure sure does get your attention.

It's Not about Hitting Bull's-Eyes

In life, all living things grow and mature. This is a natural process. But for humans, psychological growth and maturity are stunted by Reflexive Thinking. Reflexive Thinking doesn't allow you to go forward, it only permits you to go round and round, caught up in your attempts to control life. Perfectionism is the most myopic of all controlling strategies. You see only the smallest center of the target—the bull's-eye—and nothing else. And if all you see are bull's-eyes, then you're not seeing the rest of the target.

Occasional moments of success may give a false sense of security to a perfectionist: *That's it! I did it! Now all I have to do is hit another bull's-eye!* And then another, and another. However seductive the notion of being perfect may be, it's nothing more than a lifelong enslavement to control, self-loathing, and disappointment. Sure, you can feel on top of the world—as long as you're maintaining your proficiency at hitting bull's-eyes. But one miss and everything begins to crumble. For the perfectionist, a very thin line separates euphoria from chaos.

For now, engage life, shoot your arrows. If you happen to hit the target, rejoice. If you miss, learn and make adjustments. Just keep in mind that your ultimate success depends not on how many bull's-eyes you've hit today, but on what you've learned from each and *every* effort. This is where Self-Talk comes in handy.

Mirror, Mirror on the Wall

Take a look at Randy, a twenty-eight-year-old law student who went to the gym not to get into shape but, as he put it, to *sculpt* his body. Prior to his now-exhausting schedule, Randy was able to devote a few hours each day at the gym. Now, with the demands of law school, he was finding it increasingly difficult to fit in any workouts. Randy's story demonstrates the confusion and struggle that are so typical when you begin to sift through reflexive, perfectionistic thinking to get at your truth. Randy says:

> I just can't seem to let go of the feeling that all my work at the gym is being wasted. Until last month, I was in the best shape of my life. I was ripped! Now look at me. I've gained almost ten pounds, my stomach has lost its definition. . . . I feel lousy. I can't

stand the way I look. I'm trying to do what you suggested with the Self-Coaching and I think I'm progressing, but sometimes I feel so confused. There's a part of me that says: *Stop kidding yourself, just look at you. You're disgusting!*

I tried telling myself I had a choice with all of this, but no sooner did I start to challenge these thoughts than an image of me standing in front of the mirror that morning flashed through my mind. That was enough to send me over the edge. Thoughts evaporated into intense feeling, like someone punched me in the stomach. I felt nothing but a dark sadness. I couldn't get rid of that repulsive image of me standing in front of that mirror.

Fortunately, I didn't leave it there. The thought occurred to me, *If this is Reflexive Thinking, then what's the truth?* Okay, I saw that I was feeling out of control because my body was no longer perfect—not that it really was perfect, there was always something I needed to work on—but now it just seemed very . . . imperfect! That was as far as I got.

Looking back now, I realize I could have used Self-Talk and stopped contributing to these ridiculous ideas. Yeah, yeah, I was contributing to the fires of self-doubt. And yes, I know they're ridiculous—but the problem was, they didn't *feel* ridiculous when I was having them! When I step away from my insecurity, if I'm really honest with myself, I can tell you that having a perfect body isn't going to give me happiness. Why is this so hard for me to admit? But it's all so deceptive because when I'm in really good shape, I *do* feel so much better about myself. I guess what's silly is that my okayness depends on having a perfect body. I know, I know all this. I also know it's all about control. I do know . . . but for some reason I keep forgetting. Guess that's why you call this a habit.

Here's what I've come up with. I need to tell myself that if getting in shape really matters, then I will. This is the hard part: *I don't have to do it today, this instant!* Most important, I can't accept the absurd notion that having a perfect body is the answer to happiness. Sure I feel better when I look good, most people do, but for me it's not about wanting to feel better—I don't have a choice! Either I look good or I'm miserable. It feels like I'm paying extortion money to a loan shark—unless I pay the price at the gym, I can't have happiness.

Randy was beginning to see the bigger picture. Finally he was able to understand that it was never about being perfect, it was about not being able to believe in himself. Once he began to understand that perfection was nothing more than his shield against self-doubt, Randy began to develop more flexibility: "As soon as finals are over I'll find some time to work out. I'm going to risk believing that I'll get back into shape when the time comes. Hey, I'm a big boy, and if it really feels better to get back into shape, then I need to trust that's exactly what will happen. But first it's my trust muscle that needs to get exercised."

Randy's path toward happiness and contentment is no different from yours. Whatever control strategies are reflexively steering your life, you need to challenge them. Remember, insecurity is only a habit. Stop feeding and fertilizing your doubts by trying to eliminate flaws, and begin trusting that in an imperfect world, trying to be perfect is the surest way to be perfectly miserable.

Eating Disorders: The Quest for Perfect Control

The pattern of Reflexive Thinking that drove Randy toward perfection is closely related to the underlying mechanism that fuels eating disorders. Randy feared he couldn't trust himself if he began to lose control. He felt that he would abandon his focus and wind up obese and totally out of control. With most eating disorders, rigidly being able to control what is consumed becomes an emotional substitute for the inability to trust. Linda, a fourteen-year-old freshman in high school, was alarmingly thin when I met her. She was a fearful child who only wanted to feel more in control. In our first session she expressed her desire:

It's so hard for me to eat. I do try, but I'm finding it impossible. Yesterday and today I've only had a glass of juice. This is what I call a good day. When I'm able to have a good day, I feel great. Like I'm in charge and that I did a good thing. It feels so good to be able to be stronger than my hunger. I wish you could understand how important it is for me to feel strong. When I do eat, I always feel guilty. I feel heavy and ugly, but mostly like I'm a failure. I usually get very depressed and anxious. Sometimes I have scary thoughts, but that's when I begin to really watch what I eat.

Do I look good? No, I don't think so. Sure I'd like to look good, be healthy, and feel strong, but it's much more important for me to be in control. I admit there's going to be problems down the road. I always look at myself and see fat. Now it's my protruding belly. I do sit-ups, I try walking, it's just not going away. No one else sees it, but I do. I have this image of being perfectly thin. And that's all that matters. Will I ever be thin enough? I don't know. I'd rather not dwell on that. I only know I can't allow myself to gain weight.

Randy and Linda are two young people who have lost the ability to understand the distortions and danger of perfectionism. I recognize that books have been written about eating disorders, and I make no pretense about trying to do anything more than highlight the driving force behind it. Without trust, you will find a vehicle that offers the illusion of security. That vehicle is control, with a capital C. And since security is something you can't completely possess, if you're relying on calorie counting to tell you whether you're okay, you're dooming yourself to a life of constant torment and struggle—without ever really feeling okay.

Linda, like Randy, was afraid of herself. Afraid that if she didn't maintain rigid control over her eating, she would somehow turn on herself. The only solution was perfection. It was a black-and-white report card that gave her the illusion she had control over her life. Clearly it's not about her weight; it's about the desire to feel in control of life that has become unmanageable. I'm still working with Linda.

Recently we've established her reflexive tendency to see herself as someone who winds up failing, losing, or somehow being humiliated by life. Her eating disorder had become the one area of her life where she felt confidence. Our job was straightforward: Linda had to realize that controlling her weight was a metaphor for what she really needed—the ability to risk believing in herself.

We didn't approach the eating disorder directly. Rather than focusing on it as the problem, we instead began to build a foundation for recognizing the truth about herself and life. We used Self-Talk to counter the Reflexive Thinking, but mostly we built an understanding (fact from fiction) of how it wasn't about eating, it was all about control. Perfect control.

Linda wanted to be thinner; Randy wanted to lose his belly; and I, at age eleven, wanted my model to be perfect. Until we all learned the truth, it felt like we had no choice. Linda and Randy are on the road to seeing life more clearly, and I've learned to see beyond my smudges. Finally. What about you?

Self-Coaching Reflection
Security isn't a something you achieve;
it's the ongoing process of living your life
courageously and with trust.

Perfectionism: The "Unattaining State"

I'll never forget the first time I met with Sam and Diane for couples counseling. To say that Sam was impeccably dressed would be an understatement. He was about fifty years old; expensive suit; monogrammed, cuff-linked shirt; a perfect, tightly constructed Windsor knot in his tie; an obviously expensive hairpiece; and a mirror shine on his shoes. This was clearly someone who devoted time to detail. Diane was just the opposite. She was casual and relaxed in appearance, less coordinated in her outfit, and not particularly aware of her windblown hair.

Unbeknownst to Sam, Diane had taken pictures of their bedroom to show me what she referred to as her husband's "real personality." She wanted me to see his "piles" and disheveled home life. She never got the pictures out of her handbag before Sam became unhinged. Not only did he not want Diane to show me the pictures, I'm convinced he would have done whatever was necessary to prevent it. Anything! He stood up, between me and Diane, red-faced, glaring, demanding the pictures. Finally taking them from Diane, Sam declared: "If I had known you wanted to set up this meeting to smear me, I would never have agreed to come. I'll wait for you in the car." That was it. Sam walked out of the office. I never spoke a word to him.

Perfectionism comes in two varieties. The first can be seen in Sam's need to maintain a perfected image or persona for the world to see. The second, illustrated by my model experience, has more to do with an inner need or compulsion for control. So whether you are driven by what your neighbor thinks about the weeds in your lawn or by an inexplicable urge to keep the socks in your dresser lined up like soldiers, the end result is the same: a life of enslavement. Whether the motive is external and social or internal, at times your life is going to feel like a living hell.

In Dante's poetic masterpiece *The Divine Comedy* there's a place just the other side of the gates of hell for perfectionists. These are the tortured souls who must eternally pursue an unreachable banner while they are pursued by wasps and hornets that incessantly sting them. Without hope of death, these souls are caught in what was described as the "unattaining state"—desiring what can never be reached.

The "unattaining state" is where you're locked when you live a life of perfectionism. But instead of wasps and hornets, you're being constantly stung by have-tos and shoulds. If you think you can attain perfection and hold on to it, then you're still caught up in the fiction of your juggle. And you're wrong. Your liberation begins by recognizing that what you're trying to attain—perfection—isn't worth attaining. Perfection isn't as glamorous as you've made it out to be; it's nothing more than a misguided attempt to overcome insecurity. Now you know. Now you have no more excuses. Now it's a matter of Self-Talk and habit reformation.

9

No More Lies

A liar should have a good memory.
—Marcus Fabius Quintilian

When I was a kid everything seemed so clear. You did what you were told, you never answered back, and you went to church on Sundays. And then if there was any doubt, you just cracked open your little blue Baltimore Catechism for all the direction and guidance you could want. One thing that fascinated me about my moral upbringing in the Catholic Church was the notion that there were different degrees of being *bad.* According to what I remember, there are two kinds of sins, venial and mortal. Venial were minor transgressions, punishable by a visit to purgatory. Mortal—well, that was different. Committing a mortal sin would land you on the other side of the River Styx.

Growing up Catholic means not only knowing the difference between right from wrong, but knowing *how much* of a difference! This was a distinct advantage when I was young and trying to navigate through my formative years, and it's probably still a good idea now. But rather than sin, I want to apply this formula to explain another form of control, a deception we commonly refer to as lying. Like sin, lying comes in different shades: white to black. Understanding the degrees of lying can make all the difference in the world when it comes to dismantling insecurity and replacing it with a courageous attitude to be exactly who you are— the truth, the whole truth, and nothing but the truth.

Saving Your Soul

I remember a slogan from the rebellious sixties: *Peace at any cost, even if it means war.* For many, it doesn't matter how you achieve your goals, only that you do. Those who come to rely on deception as a means of control are willing to sell their psychological souls in exchange for being in control. Once this happens, their insecure lives become mere charades. They're the fakes, phonies, and frauds who, not out of maliciousness, but because of insecurity, feel they have to have control at any cost—even if it means self-degradation. Deception, like all controlling strategies, comes in many varieties. Maybe you've found yourself caught up in incessant white lies, making excuses or pretending to be someone you're not, cheating, or even manipulating. If deception has become your habit, this chapter can save your soul.

Since deception as a controlling strategy can have many expressions, use the following self-quiz to help you decide if it's a significant part your controlling juggle.

Deception Self-Quiz

Please read the following questions carefully, but don't overthink your responses. Circle your responses as being either mostly true or mostly false as they generally pertain to your life. Answer each question even if you're not completely sure. Scoring is at the end of the test.

T   F   I don't let people affect me.

T   F   I'm generally quite persuasive.

T   F   I often see people as adversaries.

T   F   I can always justify my actions.

T   F   I have a hard time admitting I've done anything wrong.

T   F   When threatened, I become shrewd and calculating.

T   F   In an argument, I'm not likely to give in.

T   F   Thinking is more valuable than feeling.

T	F	If criticized, I usually can turn things around.
T	F	You can never be too safe.
T	F	As long as I can get away with them, I have no problem telling lies.
T	F	I change so easily according to circumstances, I have a hard time knowing who I am.
T	F	I tend to be a yes-person.
T	F	I often feel disconnected from others.
T	F	I often feel like I'm an actor on a stage.
T	F	To win an argument I'll invent facts that aren't true.
T	F	I'm not very spontaneous.

A score of 0 to 4 "true" answers indicates a mild normal degree of deceptive tendencies. You'll be using this chapter more for personality expansion than for repair.

A score of 5 to 9 "true" answers indicates a moderate level of deceptive control. Your deceptions are probably undermining your capacity for effective and successful living. You can expect this chapter to significantly challenge your perceptions and experience of the world.

If you scored 10 or more "true" answers, your true sense of self has been eroded by your habit of manipulation. Your first challenge will be to restructure your thoughts and perceptions, followed by learning to risk trusting your truth. You can expect that your gains will have a major, positive impact on your life as well as on your overall happiness.

White, Gray, and Black Lying: All Part of a Continuum

Lying, simply put, is the willful substitution of fiction for fact. As you're about to find out, not all lying is problematic. In fact, some lying can be considered beneficial. The type of lying you need to be concerned with, the type driven by insecurity, can be expressed according to its destructive influence on your psychic equilibrium. The following continuum plots the three major types of lying we will focus on in this chapter.

The Lying Continuum

← ——————————————————————————————— →

White Lies	Gray Lies	Black Lies
Pleasers	*Deadbeats*	*Scammers*

White Lies: Pleasers

Lying comes in many varieties. Perhaps the most common expression is the familiar white lie. White lies are often nothing more than social lubricants: "What do you think about my hair?" asks your coworker. "Why, it looks great. It's really you," you politely reply. But if you were being totally honest, you might have said, "You poor thing! Your hair looks like the bride of Frankenstein's!" Call it what you like—being diplomatic, kind, generous, or white-lying—it's all the same thing, choosing to filter our true feelings to avoid unnecessary conflict by hurting others. And this isn't necessarily a bad thing. In fact, I shudder to think what this world would be like if everyone spoke the truth, only the truth, and nothing but the truth.

White-lying may be commonplace and innocuous when it's used to minimize social confrontation. But it can also become part of a more destructive and chronic habit of control. This happens when, not having adequate self-trust or esteem, you just can't bring yourself to tell the truth—ever. The problem is that expressing your truth, like most expressions of emotion mentioned in the previous chapter, exposes you and leaves you vulnerable to the world. For someone contorted by insecurity, this vulnerability is intolerable. When lying becomes a habit of control, you attempt to deal with a challenging situation by substituting fiction (an untruth) for fact (a truth), which ostensibly is meant to protect you from scrutiny—especially when your perception is that anyone scrutinizing you too closely would discover this terrible, empty, shell of a person.

So we see that white-lying, when driven by insecurity, isn't about genuinely wanting to help or not hurt someone by manipulating the truth, it's about controlling him or her: *If I can give you what you want, keep you from getting annoyed or angry with me, then I can control you.* Specifically, this most popular form of white-lying is the inability to say no. I describe this person as the Pleaser. Pleasers feel they have no choice: they have to please, because they have to control. But who exactly is being controlled? Sure, you're keeping the other person smiling and thinking you're terrific because you're going to drive him or her to the airport at four in the morning, but it's you who loses a night's sleep.

With white lies you try to please by saying yes when you mean no. What's the big deal? Is this really a matter for concern? This may surprise you, but being a habitual Pleaser can become a devastating form of control, one that can ruin the quality of your life. Carl's story should convince you that living a lie isn't living at all. Carl's a thirty-four-year-old physical therapist. He's a sensitive guy who just has to please:

> I guess one of my biggest problems is that I can't say no. It never seemed to be a problem, at least not until recently. I've always been popular, upbeat, everyone's friend. For the past year I've been getting more frustrated with my life—much more frustrated! Guess it hit the fan last summer when my buddy Peter asked me if I wanted to go on a cruise with him. He went on and on about this singles cruise he had heard about and how unbelievable it would be.
>
> Peter's a great guy and all, and it wasn't a terrible idea, it's just that we're really very different. He'd never know that because when I'm with him, I tend to act like him. I drink more, become more sarcastic, I even find myself acting rude and arrogant— totally out of character for me. I do it because . . . that's a good question. I guess I do it because I know Peter would put me down if I didn't. I guess that's the reason, but I'm not really sure.
>
> Anyway, the last thing I wanted to do was go on this cruise with Peter. I didn't have the time, the interest, or the money. I called to tell him my decision and found myself saying, "I'm not

sure a cruise is my thing—" Peter started to disregard everything I said, telling me, "Don't be ridiculous, this is going to be great! Trust me, you have to do this." Before I knew it, I was feeling pressured. It was just easier to say yes. Easier on the outside, but inside I was feeling trapped. *What was I doing?*

I hung up the receiver and felt a burning rage. I felt flushed, angry, out of control. I wanted to call him back and undo what had just happened. I told myself I'd calm down and call him back in the morning. The next day I called Peter back with a list of reasons why I couldn't afford to go on this cruise. Point for point, Peter began battling me, and I found myself giving in—point by point. I hung up, defeated. Now I had no choice. There was nothing left to do except pack my suitcase.

The first night on the cruise I remember thinking that maybe I was wrong and perhaps I just needed to give things a chance. Peter and I were getting ready for the opening night get-together dance at the ship's nightclub. Walking into that packed club that evening was like walking into a nightmare. There were about thirty guys and about three girls—so much for the heavily touted advertisement *Singles Extravaganza.* In that instant, the writing was on the wall: six more days, just me and Peter hanging out, drinking! By the fourth day I wanted to throw Peter overboard. We hit rough waters on the fourth night and for the rest of the cruise I was sick—I mean, really sick. I stayed in my cabin, sedated by Dramamine, boredom, and self-recrimination.

The cruise was six months ago. The only good thing about the cruise was that it opened my eyes. Since then I've become aware that I live my life doing things I don't want to do! Lately something has gone on that really concerns me. Actually, it's the reason why I decided I needed counseling. I work with another physical therapist, Helen, who is a bit pushy. Well, more than a *bit* pushy. She's a lot like Peter; let's just say she's used to getting her way. I can't say I'm afraid of her, but I do let her boss me around. She's always telling me what to do and how to do it, and I just keep smiling and nodding my head while my thoughts hover around wanting to rip her head off. I'm embarrassed to say it, but I've been bad-mouthing her to some of our clients. I know it's wrong, but I just want to get back at her.

Anyway, about a month ago I found myself beginning to dread going to work. I'd wake up feeling light-headed, faint. The tension and anxiety began to grow, especially driving to work. Lately I've been calling in sick. It really feels like I can't handle being there. Weekends I'm fine. It's just going to work that has become impossible. When I try to rationally look at what's going on, it doesn't make sense. Helen is this tiny waif of a woman, late forties—a grandmother, for God's sake! How is it possible that she can tie me up into knots? It doesn't make any sense.

Carl didn't need much coaching to convince him that enough was enough. He was fed up with himself, his life, and his pain. I started by pointing out that his Pleasing was an attempt to control through deception. And the reason situations had to be controlled was because his insecurity was telling him that the truth was too risky. I asked Carl what he thought would have happened if he had defied Peter and said no to the cruise. "Peter wouldn't have understood. He would really get fed up and let me have it." I asked, "What's the big deal if he gets fed up? And so what if he lets you have it?" Carl, scrunching up his brow, responded, "I don't know; I just can't seem to let things like that happen. I just do it." Bingo! There it was: no rational reason, only knee-jerk Reflexive Thinking. Carl needed to appreciate the fact that his habit blindly assumed that he couldn't handle conflict or confrontation.

Carl was able to trace the origins of his habit to his childhood. Being a late bloomer, he often felt inadequate and intimidated by his classmates: "I always remember being a Pleaser. I'd bring extra candy to school every day, I'd get in trouble in class just to impress the guys, I dressed like them, ate what they ate. Whatever it took, I wanted their approval." I pointed out: "It's always enlightening to know how or where these habits started, but at this point you're no longer a little boy trying to impress classmates. You're a grown man who's still *acting* like a powerless, ineffective little boy!

"Look at your reaction to Helen," I suggested. "Rather than stand up to her in a mature way, what do you do? You find a totally immature, passive-aggressive approach that tries to undermine her. It's part of a primitive, childlike reflex designed to help you escape responsibility. Because of your lack of confidence, you never learned to deal with people honestly and directly. So what happens? You, that Insecure Child habit in you, winds up getting angry at Helen—not because of what she does, but because you can't stand up to her. And since you can't be honest, you try to eliminate and destroy her by tarnishing her reputation. Clearly, we're not talking about maturity here."

The only thing preventing Carl from living more maturely was his habituated history. He needed to eliminate his Reflexive Thinking and start living in the present. He needed to reject his Reflexive Thinking habit-myth that he wasn't like everyone else, that he was inferior. Intellectually he had no trouble understanding all this, but emotionally it still *felt* like he was inferior. I laid out a Self-Coaching training plan for Carl, who couldn't wait to start experimenting.

It took only one session to get the ball rolling. It was as if a lightbulb went on in Carl's mind. He said, beaming, "That's it! That's exactly it! I can see exactly what I'm doing! I'm living a habit!" Initially he made rapid progress separating Reflexive Thinking from healthy assertions, and it wasn't long before he was looking for an opportunity to take the big plunge: risking being honest.

He didn't have to wait long for an opportunity. Peter called him that night, wanting to hang out. Carl, who had been looking forward to an easy, laid-back evening at home watching a DVD, cut Peter off: "No thanks, not tonight. I'll take a rain check." Peter, not used to being denied, persisted. But Carl was pumped up from our earlier session: "No thanks, Peter. Gotta run." Click. He did it! He said no. And guess what? The world didn't end. He actually felt good, empowered.

Carl, beginning to feel more confident, continued to fight off any and all Reflexive Thinking impulses to needlessly acquiesce to others. It helped Carl to refer to his Reflexive Thinking as his Insecure Child. Visualizing himself shuffling his feet and acting like he was ten years old was all he needed to start being more effective—and mature. As he began to accumulate some valuable experience, Carl realized that his ability to risk being honest wasn't as difficult or as far-fetched as he imagined. Without the Reflexive Thinking feelings of victimization, without passive-aggressive anger, Carl was amazed to find out just how easy it was to look someone in the eye, with compassion, honesty, and maturity, and simply tell that person no. "I can't believe it. It's really not that hard to say no. Guess it was that ice-breaking first step that was the hardest, because, tell you the truth, it's been easy ever since." Carl finally left his feelings of inferiority where they belonged, in his history.

Gray Lies: Deadbeats

As we continue along our continuum we now move from the white lie, which can be described merely as a social lubricant, to another form of lying, which can best be described as a social friction. This is the realm of the Deadbeat. A Deadbeat will promise you the world, but what you wind up with won't be the world, just more of those empty promises: "I know I promised to get the job done. Just give me one more week. I promise, one more week." Deadbeats tend to be Pleasers as well as manipulators. That's why they can be slippery characters who can rationalize away any and all negatives. Deadbeats can be so convincing, they often wind up believing their own lies.

If you happen to have the misfortune to be married to a Deadbeat, you know all too well how frustrating this can be. Nancy, a thirty-six-year-old stay-at-home mom, thought her head was going to explode:

> Living with Mike is driving me to drink! I just feel like I'm always getting bamboozled. If I think we should put a rug in the living room, he'll have no problem promising me that we'll go shopping. Do we get the rug? No! And no matter what I try to do or say,

145

there's always an excuse or one of his famous reasons for why "not now." It seems impossible for him to give in on anything. Eventually he wears me down. I'm not sure how he does this. Maybe I just give up or maybe he makes me doubt my own perceptions. He always manages to get away with anything he doesn't want to do. And I'm not happy about it.

Ever since we were married, Mike's been promising to take the family to Disney World. I've been patient, and now we can afford it. All of a sudden Mike tells me Disney World isn't a good idea. He's heard something about terrorist threats and thinks it's not safe. Trust me, I know this isn't the reason. I overheard him talking with his brother about renting a house with him at the Jersey shore for a couple of weeks. Anyway, I didn't let on to him that I heard his conversation, and I insisted that I wanted to go to Disney. Mike said he'd think about it.

As the weeks went by it seemed that Mike was making it a point of letting me know how terrible the world situation was becoming, how many of his coworkers weren't planning on flying or traveling far from home. In spite of what I knew he was trying to do, I found myself thinking that what he was saying made sense. After all, maybe I was just being pigheaded not to consider the dangers. I tried not to give in, but in the end, I folded. He was able to convince me that I would be a nervous wreck if we went to Disney.

What's funny is that if for any reason Mike were to change his mind and want to fly to Disney, I know he would be able to convince me that my fears were unfounded. We would be on our way. Mike just has a way of bending me in his direction. He may be getting what he wants, but why does he always get my hopes up and then disappoint me? For once I'd like to call the shots.

As you can see, Deadbeats are crafty manipulators. Mike may be winning the battle as to where the family vacations this summer, but he may be jeopardizing his marriage. If you find yourself trying to control others by lying, pleasing, or making idle promises, it's time for you to see if insecurity's manipulating you! Ask yourself: *Am I able to be more flexible? Do I have problems with normal give-and-take? What about separating fact from fiction?* Or worse, *Do I treat fiction as if it were a fact? Do I feel that my view usually prevails? Or should I say, has to prevail? In a pinch, am I willing to say almost anything to maintain control?*

Black Lies: Scammers

The opposite pole to white-lying is black-lying. With black lies, we've gone beyond social lubricant or social friction and entered the realm of social mauling. Black-lying isn't innocent; it's malicious and usually it's deliberate. Scamming is a common example. Someone who scams is looking to pull the wool over your eyes to trick, deceive, or otherwise control you. Such people are persuasive, cunning, clever, and often quite devious. They'll look you in the eye and tell you that they only care about your well-being, while behind that cheap facade is a calculating, manipulating coldness.

Scamming, especially in its more subtle expressions, may easily be overlooked. You need to ask yourself: "Do I tend to manipulate the truth to prevail?" If so, you're going to need to do a quick reality check; if you don't, you're in jeopardy of losing your moral compass. And once this happens you're going to have a hard time feeling good about yourself or your life.

Rosemary, a thirty-seven-year-old pharmaceutical salesperson, had the misfortune of being sold a bill of goods by a crafty—and altogether despicable—Scammer:

> I met Stanley at a singles weekend last month. It was an instant connection. The whole weekend, we couldn't keep our eyes off each other—or our hands. When we got back from the weekend,

Stanley would call me two, three times a day, telling me that he was crazy about me and how he's been looking for someone like me all his life. Coming off a breakup of a three-year relationship, I was vulnerable and susceptible to his words. He sent me flowers, cards, e-mails—I was reeling.

We went out to dinner the following Friday night. It was wonderfully romantic. Stanley told me not to be offended, that he was a man of strong instinct and intuition and knew that what he felt for me was more than attraction. He told me that, as crazy as it sounded, he had fallen in love with me! I remember feeling goose bumps hearing those words. Of course, it couldn't possibly be true—this was only our first official date—but it still felt glorious to hear him say it. And why not? Stanley was handsome, romantic, charming, everything I was missing in my previous relationship. I was melting.

On the way home that night Stanley was talking about the future—our future! Can you believe it? He was talking about one day getting engaged, moving in together, he was so energetic, so convincing. I invited him in for a drink. I don't usually do that, but I just couldn't let go of the night. After a few glasses of wine, we made passionate love all night.

That was Friday, a month ago! I haven't heard from Stanley since. He doesn't return my calls or e-mails. I feel so used, so manipulated. How could he do this to me?

It's not hard to do if you're a Scammer. For a Scammer, it's a no-holds-barred attitude when it comes to controlling a situation. Facts are no obstacle, not when they can be ignored or manipulated. Remember the children's story about the ant and the grasshopper? It went something like this: There was once an ant who worked very hard, day and night in the withering summer heat, building his house and laying up supplies for the winter. Meanwhile, the wily grasshopper, thinking the ant a fool, chose instead to laugh and dance and plays the summer away. Come winter, the ant is warm and well fed. The grasshopper has no food or shelter, so he dies out in the cold.

The moral of the story doesn't escape any child: *You reap what you sow.* But for a Scammer, who can argue any side of an argument, things can easily be inverted, black to white, white to black. After all, why should the ant be allowed to be warm and well fed while less fortunate grasshoppers are cold and starving? From Stanley's point of view, why shouldn't he try to seduce Rosemary? If Stanley is any kind of a Scammer, he probably sees it all as a game. He played his cards right and won.

Is it so terrible to occasionally say whatever it takes to get your way? The answer is a resounding *yes!* This type of nefarious deception will eventually leave you emotionally bankrupt and morally running on empty. There's no two ways about it; it's a shabby defense reserved only for shabby individuals. After all, what do you expect when the only thing that matters is personal gain at the expense of others?

✤ ✤ ✤

SELF-COACHING POWER DRILL

Look at the following exercise to see if you can isolate any white (Pleaser), gray (Deadbeat), or black (Scammer) lying within yourself. For each of the following six scenarios, circle the answer or answers that best describe how you might handle the situation (the answers follow the sixth scenario). As you will see, it's not unusual for there to be overlap when trying to discern these strategies of deception. This drill will help you develop more consciousness and awareness.

1. You've just been asked to go to dinner with someone you don't particularly like. Do any of the following responses describe how you might respond?
   a. "Can't go tonight, but give me a call and let's definitely try to connect next week." *She must be crazy thinking I would actually go to dinner with her!*

b. "Sure I'll go." *I can't stand her, but what's the difference? It's just a few hours.*

c. "I'm sorry, I'm not up for dinner. I have this terrible headache, I feel so sick. But since you're offering, would you mind picking something up for me on the way home and dropping it off?" *So I don't have a headache, no big deal. At least now I can go home and watch my TV show and not have to worry about fixing dinner.*

2. You're up for a promotion, but you fear that your coworker Sally may get the nod before you. Imagine that you're talking with your boss. Do any of the following statements sound like anything you might say?

a. "Sally's a great worker; too bad she's not happy with the company." *Hey, I'm entitled to my opinion, even if it's not true.*

b. "Did I ever mention to you that I would be finishing up my college degree this year?" *He'll never find out I didn't go to college.*

c. "Is there anything else I can do for you? I'm free this weekend, I'll be glad to come in." *Hey, whatever it takes. I need this promotion. Let's just hope he doesn't call my bluff.*

3. You just met another parent from your daughter's school and you'd like to leave a good impression. Can you imagine yourself responding like any of the following?

a. "Me? I'm a writer. A few publishers have expressed interest in my latest project." *Well, it's true I want to be a writer. What's the harm in puffing myself up a bit?*

b. "If ever you or your daughter need a ride to school, just let me know. I can imagine how busy you are. Just let me know if I can help out." *I'm sure that got me a few brownie points.*

c. "If ever you or your daughter need a ride to school, just let me know." *Yeah, like I'm really going to be your taxi service!*

4. You've just been pulled over by a police officer for speeding. How might you see yourself responding?

a. "I'm sorry, Officer. You're perfectly in the right to pull me over. I respect the difficult job you guys have to do." *Idiot! Please, please don't give me a ticket!*

b. "I'm so sorry, Officer. I've been so distraught lately, ever since my mother went into the hospital." *Actually, I'm distraught because I'm not going to get home in time to see my favorite TV program.*

c. "Please forgive me, Officer. If you could just let me go this one time, I guarantee I'll never do this again. I'm not just saying that, I really mean it. Can you give me a break?" *What else can I do? I'd offer him a bribe if I didn't feel I'd get in trouble.*

5. Your partner just found out you've been cheating. Which best describes how you might respond?

   a. "You've got to trust me. This won't ever happen again, I promise." *Yeah, I promise to be more careful in the future.*

   b. "No, it's not what you think. I was just helping someone who was going through some tough times." *Yeah, right!*

   c. "You know I love only you. This affair means absolutely nothing to me. You know I have a drinking problem. I just had too much to drink, that's all. I promise it will never happen again. I'm going to an AA meeting tomorrow night." *Well, maybe not tomorrow night. But someday I'll go. Maybe.*

6. You're running out of time; you have a report due and your boss just called and wants to know what's going on. How might you handle this crisis?

   a. "Whatever you want, just say the word and I'll stay here all night if I have to." *She's being ridiculous, but what choice do I have?*

   b. "Just give me another week; I promise you'll have it on your desk by Monday. I know I told you that last week, but I really mean it this time." *Well, I probably mean it.*

   c. "I've been feeling really ill lately: I think it's my gall bladder. In fact, I have an appointment with the doctor tomorrow.

Can you give me an extension?" *That was convincing; now I hope she doesn't ask me to bring a doctor's note.*

1. Response a—Deadbeat; Pleaser
   Response b—Pleaser
   Response c—Scammer
2. Response a—Scammer
   Response b—Scammer
   Response c—Pleaser; Deadbeat
3. Response a—Scammer
   Response b—Pleaser
   Response c—Pleaser; Deadbeat
4. Response a—Pleaser; Scammer
   Response b—Pleaser; Scammer
   Response c—Pleaser; Deadbeat
5. Response a—Deadbeat; Scammer
   Response b—Scammer
   Response c—Scammer; Deadbeat
6. Response a—Pleaser
   Response b—Deadbeat
   Response c—Scammer

10

Trust Yourself

I've never been one to sit around watching the grass grow. I've always been busy, always going somewhere and doing something. At some point in my early life, this rather natural, energetic disposition became connected to insecurity. At that point, what was energetic and spontaneous was detoured into a life of control, worry, anxiety, and frustration, capped by a series of dead-end jobs and uncertainty about going back to school. In spite of (or more likely because of) my anxiety and insecurity, I found myself attracted to the field of psychology. It seemed to me that I could kill a couple of birds with one stone: pursue a respectable career in psychology while simultaneously figuring out how to feel better about my own life. I'm not sure which of the two reasons was my prime mover, but I suspect it was the latter. If there was a secret to a successful and happy life, I was going to find it.

Like a lot of people, I had wasted a good deal of time looking in all the wrong places as I chased money, status, control, and other short-sighted goals that left me with nothing more than a growing sense of disappointment and skepticism. Was happiness just an illusion? My many years of studying, training, and private practice paid off, teaching me two important things: that happiness and success aren't illusions; and yes, there is a secret. Well, not exactly a secret, it was more of a realization that a successful and happy life depends on one's ability for self-trust. The secret is self-trust!

Trust Self-Quiz

The following questions are geared to help you understand the different ways trust can be undermined. Please read the questions carefully, but don't overthink your responses. Circle your responses as being either mostly true or mostly false as they generally pertain to your life. Answer each question even if you're not completely sure. Scoring is at the end of the test.

T	F	I usually distrust my decisions.
T	F	I'm generally afraid to take risks.
T	F	I worry that what I say to others isn't acceptable.
T	F	I'm too cautious.
T	F	I expect things to go wrong.
T	F	I don't trust my opinions.
T	F	I usually don't trust my feelings.
T	F	I can't change.
T	F	I have a hard time trusting fate.
T	F	I worry about my health.
T	F	I don't trust my impulses.
T	F	I usually distrust others.
T	F	I don't handle challenges well.
T	F	I always need to be in control.
T	F	I fear flying (elevators, bridges, etc.).
T	F	I usually don't believe what people tell me.
T	F	I'm suspicious of people's motives.
T	F	You never can be too safe.
T	F	In relationships, I tend to be jealous.
T	F	I'm much more of a thinker than a doer.

These questions are to help orient you to the expressions of distrust in your life. Although any distrust is too much, a score of 7 or fewer "true" responses suggests that you have a satisfactory quality of life.

Self-Coaching can teach you to cultivate an even deeper awareness, spontaneity, and enjoyment of life.

A score of 8 to 13 suggests that the quality of your life is significantly restricted by an inability to trust. For you, it's safe to assume that Self-Coaching will make a profound difference in your overall happiness.

A score of 14 or more suggests that the quality of your life is substantially compromised by insecurity and distrust. Self-Coaching can make a profound difference in the quality of your life.

Self-Coaching Reflection
A successful life depends on a foundation
of self-trust.

What is self-trust? Simply put, self-trust is a willingness to believe in yourself. The key is understanding that a willingness to believe implies some degree of risk. To trust, you must learn to risk trusting. Your biggest obstacle will be your insecurity and Reflexive Thinking telling you you're crazy to stop worrying, rehearsing, or manipulating life, insisting that if you were to let go of control, life as you know it would crumble. It's not unusual to become intimidated by this threat. That's why you need a program such as Self-Coaching to teach and motivate you to reject insecurity once and for all and replace it with a willingness to believe in yourself.

With adequate self-trust you bring all of yourself forward, not just the narrow focus of ego consciousness (i.e., your stream-of-consciousness thinking) that is so typical of someone caught up in one of life's control juggles. Although it took me years of trial and error to teach myself to self-trust, I've managed to synthesize what I've learned into the simple, straightforward program that you now hold in your hands. Once you become armed with an understanding of the reflexive habits that have detoured you from the life you want, *The Power of Self-Coaching* will provide the necessary tools that will enable you to abandon self-doubt, insecurity, and control—and replace them with self-trust.

Self-trust taught me to experience my own anxiety-prone disposition not as the tightening noose I once felt, but as a catalyst for a more natural life filled with energy, passion, and interest. What you feel to be a negative limitation or frustration in your life may be negative only because insecurity is clouding the picture, filling you with fear and hesitation. I can show you how, with a little insight and some Self-Coaching, those negatives can be transposed into positives. And why not? After all, your insecurity was learned, so it can be unlearned.

❖ ❖ ❖

SELF-COACHING POWER DRILL

To separate yourself from the contaminating effects of Reflexive Thinking, I'd suggest a very simple drill that can provide powerful insights. Start by creating an image of a person (real or imagined) who portrays strong qualities of self-trust. This needs to be a confident, self-assured person who handles life without hesitation or doubt. This personification is called your trust persona. Or, if you prefer, you can choose any person you know or admire who represents trust and confidence. As long as your trust persona represents someone other than yourself—the ego identity you're identified with.

Depending on your own level of insecurity, it may be a challenge for you to generate an image of a strong, confident trust persona, but don't give up. Creating a trust persona is more important than you may realize. The mere fact that you're conjuring up such a mental image means you'll be awakening this potential within you. You wouldn't be able to create the fantasy if it weren't so. So from now on, every time you find yourself slipping into doubt or distrust, get used to asking: *How would my trust persona handle this?* By removing yourself from your typical Reflexive Thinking and depersonalizing the image, you can get an uncontaminated, oftentimes unexpected response. The key to this drill depends not on asking how *you* should handle difficulty, but on how your trust persona would handle it.

❖ ❖ ❖

Running on Empty

Why is a natural life of self-trust more effective than, say, a life of workaholism or compulsion? I was asked this question the other day by Erin, a distraught thirty-nine-year-old woman I was working with. She was driving herself into the ground because the only thing she had to show for her life of compulsive scrambling was a case of chronic frustration. As you are about to see, Erin's struggle is rather classic and will serve as a suitable model to help you further understand just how important self-trust can be in turning your life around, especially if you feel you've been emotionally running on empty.

Everything from not being able to hold down a job, to watching her friends succeed, marry, and start families was beginning to stir up an uncomfortable panic deep within Erin. "It just seems impossible now. I should have stayed in school. Now I don't have a degree, I have no practical skills, no direction, no job, and my hair is already turning gray! Doc, don't you understand? I can't afford to let things unfold naturally! I'm running out of time!"

Erin's chronic agitation was because she couldn't trust herself or her life; nothing was ever good enough. When things were good, she would invariably find fault because they weren't perfect enough, or because her doubts convinced her that she was deluding herself. When she was in college, her high school friends were making more money, driving beautiful cars, and taking exotic vacations. So as not to lose any more ground, Erin quit school and started working. After a few frustrating years of never "making it," she realized that other friends, who did remain in school, were graduating and becoming doctors and lawyers. Erin, already floundering and panicked in her workaday world, went back to school and started all over. Again! Truth was, it didn't matter what she did; Erin always saw herself on the opposite side of the fence from success. And, as you know, the grass always seems greener on the other side.

With inadequate self-trust, you, like Erin, are left with only one recourse. Rather than living life naturally and spontaneously, you must seek a life of control. And as you've learned, the habits of control and Reflexive Thinking offer at best only a temporary illusion of security.

What's worse is that the psychic energy used to fuel a life of control is always siphoned away from your natural ability to trust yourself: the more control you seek, the more you deplete your ability to trust. Erin came into therapy with her trust tank almost emptied; that's why she was so desperate.

Lack of Trust: It's Unnatural

Erin was an overthinker, a person who tries too hard to figure out life rather than live it. Every thought and every decision mattered too much. "What if I make a mistake?" "What if I change my mind?" Those damned what-ifs! Since Erin's real inclinations and intuitions were obscured by her insecurity and distrust, by default she resorted to a pressure cooker life of control. Reflexive Thinking left her congested not only with incessant what-ifs but also with a tendency to make endless debasing comparisons: "I saw this woman driving a big Mercedes today . . . the fur she was wearing probably cost a thousand dollars. I don't even have a coat that fits, much less a car. I started thinking about her house in the suburbs, her husband, kids . . . I'm so embarrassed."

Erin's life had become nothing more than a blur of confused thoughts, fears, and regrets. There wasn't anything natural about her constant obsessive thoughts or wasteful pursuits. The more pressure Erin felt, the more frantic she became, and the more frantic, the more disoriented. Her natural strengths and inclinations were completely overshadowed by her anxiety and growing depression. Without self-trust, nothing natural—nothing inherently satisfying—could take root. In Erin's life nothing was ever good enough.

Erin's biggest problem was that long ago she had sold out her ability to believe in herself. A combination of a mild learning disability and ensuing feelings of inadequacy had convinced her at an early age that she wasn't as good as everybody else. Because of the way she processed information, it was difficult for Erin to articulate her thoughts quickly and coherently. As she began to struggle, anxiety and fear entered the equation and left her tormented. Here's what she told me:

Every time I opened my mouth, I never knew what would come

out. Sometimes I couldn't find the right word; at other times I just felt this terrible pressure. I tried so hard not to mess up. I think that's what got me into trouble. Rather than studying more, I would try to figure out how to get around feeling embarrassed. Early on I became the class clown and would wind up at the principal's office regularly. Kids seemed to like me, but everything else was deteriorating. My teachers told my parents how intelligent I was and that I was just being lazy. At the time I felt they were saying I was smart just to motivate me, but I wasn't falling for it, I knew the real truth! The truth was that I was far from smart—hell, I couldn't even think straight!

Erin's doubts led to an erosion of self-trust that only became amplified as she grew up. That's why nothing was ever good enough. She couldn't, for example, follow a simple inclination or impulse, because immediately she would be bombarded with fifteen competing reasons why she should be trying something more lucrative. It's not uncommon for someone with insecurity to flitter butterflylike through life from one experience to the next, hoping against hope to find the perfect answer.

Self-Coaching Reflection
Time to kill the Buddha

There's a Zen adage that goes, "If you meet the Buddha on the road, kill him." If lack of self-trust is driving you from one disappointment to the next, I suggest you consider this adage carefully. According to Buddhist philosophy, the Buddha represents enlightenment and must be found within you. So if you happen to be walking along the road one day and run into the Buddha, beware! Since no upstanding Buddha can come from outside yourself, you will know that this must be a false Buddha (a false truth). Killing the Buddha means killing your false, insecurity-driven, external pursuits. This sounds rather violent, but keep in mind that false truths are killing your life right now!

❖ ❖ ❖

Erin and I started with some really simple Self-Coaching drills. I wanted Erin to become more courageous with a few simple leaps of faith, such as choosing what to order at a restaurant or what movie to see. I challenged her: "You have much more to gain by going with your inclination and winding up with a meal that may not be perfect than if you continue to insist you have to know everything in advance. Your compulsion not to make any mistakes is killing you. You've become so distrustful you doubt everything. It's the doubt that's eroding your life and leaving you sunk in confusion and despair."

❖ ❖ ❖

SELF-COACHING POWER DRILL

Like Erin, you need to begin taking some simple leaps of faith. You need to understand that your inability to trust reflects nothing more than years of neglect. Years when rather than trusting your natural, spontaneous instincts and intuitions, you allowed yourself to be swayed by the congested thinking of insecurity. Instead of putting your faith where it belonged—in you—you convinced yourself that controlling life was the answer. And you've been handing your life over to Reflexive Thinking ever since. Bottom line: your trust muscle has atrophied and needs a bit of resuscitation.

Let's begin this muscle-building with a few simple and safe challenges. These can be anything: what color outfit to wear, when to return a phone call, or what TV show to watch, as long as it involves the need for a choice. Once you have your challenge in front of you, I'd like you to be *daring*. (Remember that these are inconsequential choices. For now, *do not* apply this drill to significant problems or challenges.) Just allow yourself to go with your first gut impulse. Don't overthink it, just do it! Get used to taking the brake off and finding out what happens.

At first, being spontaneous may feel downright reckless! That's okay; you're worth the risk. Keep in mind it only *feels* reckless in contrast to your overly controlled, reflexive lifestyle. Eventually you'll find that living more spontaneously feels absolutely exhilarating. The essence of this drill is to get you to shake off the rigid

adherence to Reflexive Thinking and replace it with a spontaneity of reacting. The goal isn't to become a nonthinker; you just
need to be convinced there's more to life than control thinking.
To get balance and trust back into your life, you're going to need
to let *all* of your personality fly.

Truth vs. Fiction

Erin worked hard at changing her incessant need to compare herself to
others and, of course, her chronic distrust. She began to realize the
habitual nature of these tendencies, and finally recognized that the only
reason she couldn't trust herself was because she was afraid to risk it;
fear, not fact, was dictating. Deep down, Erin was sure she was inferior
to everyone else, but somehow had to figure out how to pull a fast one
so no one would see that she was a failure. This is what insecurity
does—it creates a fiction. In Erin's fiction she was her own albatross
hanging around her own neck, forever damned to inferiority.

A personal fiction can't stand up against the truth—not for long,
especially if you're willing to challenge it. (In the next part of this book
you're going to learn a powerful technique called Self-Talk, which will
allow you to challenge any fiction, no matter how resistant or how long-
standing.) Erin proved to be tenacious with her Self-Coaching. She pro-
gressed to larger decisions and bigger risks. Eventually she took the
ultimate risk: insisting that she was okay. It was the ultimate risk to bring
out the ultimate truth. From this point on, Erin's life began to soar.

Erin found out that she always loved the outdoors. She had dismissed
a career with the National Park Service years ago because it didn't meet
with her calculations of financial success or the image of the well-dressed
Madison Avenue type. She had never allowed herself to pursue such
a simple dream because she had too much ground to make up. Erin
had been aware of her dream but had hit the brakes on it quickly. "I had
to be more successful than that," she said. She had to be more successful because her personal fiction would never let her rest: she had to
keep everyone away from her secret that she wasn't okay. Insecurity,

not Erin, was steering the course of her life straight into a brick wall.

Self-Coaching taught Erin that she no longer had to be the passenger in this collision of a life, that, with adequate self-trust, she could take the wheel and steer her life wherever she wanted. How significant was Erin's shift? As Robert Frost wrote in his poem "The Road Less Traveled," "And that has made all the difference." Erin reentered college, this time in a forestry program, and this time with an attitude of self-assurance and calm. Currently she's working hard to meet tuition payments, but happier and more content than she's ever been in her life. I recently got a postcard from Erin, who was vacationing in Yellowstone National Park. She wrote, "I was afraid to be happy because I thought I might regret it. *I don't!*"

Self-Coaching Reflection
Unless your habits of insecurity are broken,
they will follow you through life.

Once you learn to break the habits of insecurity and allow self-trust to emerge, your worry, rumination, fear, and hesitation quickly recede as you begin finding out how effortless life can become.

Self-Coaching Reflection
The buck stops with you—take responsibility for your success.

Just as a baseball player's success isn't reflected by one or two turns at bat but by his cumulative batting average, it's never one experience that dictates your fate. It's the accumulation of all your life experiences, along with your interpretation of these experiences, that determines the life you wind up with. And make no mistake: recognizing and trusting your truth is the only way to turn the tide of your life experience from struggle to success. It's up to you—no one else.

Self-Coaching Reflection
life experience + self-trust = success
life experience + insecurity = struggle

PART III

The Five Steps of Self-Talk

Self-Talk in Five Steps

Part II was specifically designed to build a foundation of understanding and consciousness—to educate you as to why you're struggling with life. Now that you're familiar with the effects that insecurity, control, distrust, and Reflexive Thinking can have on your life, you're ready for Self-Coaching's five-step program for change. Just five simple, practical, but essential steps to creating a life that not only makes more sense, but also, until now, that you've only dreamed of having.

The five steps that you are about to learn comprise a powerful technique I call Self-Talk. Although Self-Talk was first introduced in my previous book, the version you're about to learn bears little resemblance to the original. Having gone through many significant revisions these past few years, what has emerged is a much more evolved and powerful technique. Essentially Self-Talk is a way for you to learn to become an active participant in your own thinking. Rather than passively being led around by Reflexive Thinking, Self-Talk puts you in the driver's seat, where you decide who's going to be steering your thoughts—you or insecurity. And with this kind of power you can begin to create exactly the life you want.

11

Step One:
Chart Your Weaknesses

I had an old sports car that had a bit of a quirk. Every time it rained, if I were making a hard left turn, it would stall. Going straight or making right turns never seemed to affect it! For months my mechanic and I scratched our heads over this pattern. It just didn't make any sense. Since I wasn't in a position to buy another car, I had to manage as best I could with my aquatic woes. Whenever it rained I tried to avoid—as much as possible—left-hand turns. When there wasn't a choice, I would enter a turn barely moving (much to the annoyance of the drivers behind me). After a while I managed never to stall out again. I came to anticipate and overcome my car's temperamental pattern.

Eventually I found a mechanic who solved the mystery. Seems there was a crack in the left-side wheel well, and every time I would make a left-hand turn, water would splash from the tires into the crack, where it found and saturated a stripped electrical wire, causing a short. I mention my car because—until you make the necessary changes in your life—it's important to anticipate where your weak points are so you don't stall out or otherwise get into trouble. Your Self-Talk training begins with Step One, where you will learn to assess the habits of control that have short-circuited your life. Being able to anticipate these habits is the first step toward breaking the grip of Reflexive Thinking and recognizing that you have a choice to create whatever life you want.

Step One also is meant to be diagnostic. Let me explain. With my car, once my mechanic was able to locate the trouble, the turning mystery could be solved and eliminated. Once you have an accurate diagnosis of your controlling habits, you'll have the foundation necessary to launch your Self-Talk efforts to solve and eliminate any struggle. It all begins with an accurate appraisal of your weaknesses.

Solving the Puzzle

Imagine yourself sitting in front of a thousand-piece jigsaw puzzle. Where to begin? You might begin by looking at the picture on the box lid—a small seaport; some fishing boats; a pier; a few small shacks; and there, off to one side, you notice a bright red rowboat. That's it: that's how you'll begin your assault on the puzzle. You sift through the jungle of pieces until you spot one with a splash of red, then another, and so on.

When I sit down with someone in therapy, I approach them in the same way, only instead of looking for a bright red rowboat, I'm hunting for telltale expressions of control. If you learn to look for patterns of control (see the list that follows) as the focal point to understanding your struggle, then, rather than being confused, you will be on your way to solving the puzzle that has become your life. Step One will help you accomplish this.

People I work with are often amazed at how easily I seem to be able to make sense of problems that have confounded them for years. But once I teach them to see their own control tendencies—their own bright red rowboats—they understand just how straightforward this understanding can be. Sure, you may struggle or stumble as you begin to break these habits of control—all habits are resistant to change. But I guarantee, once you're fortified with a firm understanding of how you allowed yourself to be duped, you'll no longer be blind. You'll know what's necessary to liberate yourself from the restrictions imposed by Reflexive Thinking and insecurity. For now, your first step to creating the life you want is to articulate what your control tendencies are.

Charting Your Control Tendencies

Controlling strategies can be very diverse, ranging from simple expressions such as those of stubbornness and negativity—"No, I won't go"—to more intense and debilitating expressions, such as the immobilizing feelings associated with panic attacks. Although there are endless creative possibilities, here is a list of control's more typical expressions, which will assist you in making an assessment of your own unique habits of control. The following are the most common expressions of control. Make note of your tendencies:

Yes, buts

"*Yes,* I didn't get the job finished, *but* I couldn't help getting sick." A yes-but strategy allows you to sidestep responsibility by first feigning blame. "Yes, I took your money," only to sidestep it with a rationalization, "But I wasn't stealing it, I was just borrowing it." If you're impervious to criticism, you're in complete control.

Have-tos

"I have to be the best." Or, "I have to lie; she would never be able to handle the truth." Have-tos are compulsive strategies designed to help you control others and life. Once you become convinced that you *have* to do something, you can eliminate all doubt.

Worrying or what-iffing

"What if I fail?" Or, "What if he says no?" Worry is an attempt to eliminate doubt by trying to know what's coming before it arrives. In spite of the fact that no one knows the future, you keep telling yourself that if you can just figure out what's going to happen (i.e., worry), you'll be able to brace yourself and be more adequately prepared.

Can'ts

"I can't handle that job." Or, "I can't relax." When you say "I can't . . ." you're giving up in order to feel more in control. Once you conclude that you *can't*, you've just excused yourself from any struggle or possible failure. If you avoid failure, you're in control.

Guilts

"I have to go; she'll be mad if I don't." Guilt is a powerful emotion that tries to keep you from going against someone or something. You're trying to avoid feeling that you did something wrong. If you allow guilt to pressure you into doing what's expected, then you maintain control by avoiding conflict. If, on the other hand, you do go against someone, guilt offers a repentant, often anguished reaction meant to restore control. "I'm sorry, I'll never do that to you again."

Black-and-white thinking

Black-and-white thinking is "all-or-none" thinking—never is there any gray or middle ground. If you can convince yourself that something is either black or white, you're done. Case closed. No more discussion. In control.

Doubts

"Maybe I shouldn't call her. How do I know she won't be angry?" Doubts act as a brake trying to postpone, avoid, or somehow protect you from perceived danger. You're trying to control by slowing down and not being too hasty. Inertia is safer than making a mistake.

Shoulds

Shoulds are similar to have-tos. Both are compulsive strategies by which you attempt to control life. Shoulds are more closely related to guilt and societal expectations.

Name-calling

"I'm such a idiot!" Putting yourself down is a cheap way of excusing yourself from conflict. After all, you can't really expect an "idiot" to handle life.

Not caring

"I don't care if I upset her." Not caring is a form of denial. If you can insulate yourself with callousness, you can remain in control—even if you mess up.

Hostility

"As far as I'm concerned, you can go straight to hell." Hostility repels. By pushing someone away, you create an insulation between you and that person. Insulation is control.

Lying
Why take any responsibility when you can control others by lying? If one reality doesn't suit you, create another with lies.

Manipulating
People are malleable—a little white lie here, a bit of coercion there, and perhaps some feigned hysterics—these are all useful tools if you're trying to twist someone to your will. If you can manipulate others, you control them and the situation.

Mountain-out-of-molehill generalizing
Generalizing is an attempt to prepare for the worst. If something is catastrophic and you anticipate it, then you're not going to be unprepared. It's all about not being caught off guard and unaware. If the world is ending, you damn well better know about it so you can get ready.

Fatalistic thinking/doom and gloom
With mountain-out-of-molehill thinking, you're at least trying to prepare for and defend yourself from adversity. With fatalistic thinking, you've already concluded the worst and you throw your hands up, becoming victimized, powerless, and impotent. You can feel a sense of control when you don't have to struggle any longer.

From the above, see if you can begin to compile a list of the controlling tendencies that make up your unique controlling juggle. It helps to visualize yourself with several balls in hand, struggling to juggle these tendencies in your life. You may, for example, react to one situation with charm and manipulation, another with hostility and aggression, while another with isolation and withdrawal. All are control strategies designed to protect you from life—the life your insecurity has convinced you that you can't handle. If you recall from your reading, juggling—any kind of juggling—inevitably becomes a struggle as you grow tired, trying desperately to prevent a collapse.

Making It Visual

My wife's a kindergarten teacher who long ago taught me the value of making concepts visual. Now, whenever I give a talk, I use plenty of metaphors, allusions, and expansive gestures. It really helps to try to visualize what your mind is trying to grasp. That's why I'm going to ask you to use the following exercise to both plot and visualize your habits of control. You'll be amazed how much easier it is to keep things straight when you can see them written on the page rather than just think about them in your head.

1. On a blank sheet of paper and using the above list of common expressions as a general guide, draw a few circles. These will represent the balls you use in your juggle. Write each control tendency you experience in a different circle. See how many balls you can identify for yourself. I suggest that you draw larger circles for your more dominant tendencies and smaller circles for weaker tendencies.

2. As you progress with your Self-Coaching program, be sure to add or remove balls as you gain insights and make life changes.

Plotting Your Reflexive Thinking

As you continue to build visual expressions, I'd like to help you construct a composite picture of your reflexive habits of control along with the intensity of the struggle associated with them. On the following continuum, one side represents mature, Healthy Thinking and the opposite side represents insecure, Reflexive Thinking. Depending on the severity of your particular symptoms, you will notice that some thoughts tend to lean in the direction of Healthy Thinking, while other thoughts may lean toward Reflexive Thinking.

Go back to the list of controlling strategies that you just compiled as part of your juggle; then, using the descriptions given in the following key, estimate the point or points on the continuum that reflect the extent of Reflexive Thinking associated with each these habits. Keep in mind that the continuum is only meant to be an intuitive approximation; you don't have to worry about precision. The goal is to create a visual estimate of your Reflexive Thinking habits. The ability to see these tendencies graphically can be a powerful tool in helping you avoid confusion as we proceed with your Self-Coaching training.

Also, recall from the previous exercise that you were instructed to draw larger circles for your more dominant controlling tendencies and smaller circles for weaker tendencies. Use the continuum below to assist you with these drawings. Scoring follows the continuum.

Control Juggling/Reflexive Thinking (RT)

1	2 3 4 5 6 7	8 9 10 11 12 13	14 15 16 17 18 19	20
Healthy Thinking	mild–moderate RT	moderate RT	moderate–severe RT	severe RT

Reflexive Thinking/severe impairment (score of 20). Symptoms/habits that occur at this level of impairment lead to a complete shutdown of your ability to handle any life demands.

Typical symptoms at this level may include severe depression, severe anxiety and panic, suicide potential, chronic daily substance abuse, inability to work or socialize, chronic physical ailments, and need for hospitalization.

Control juggling/moderate–severe impairment (score of 14 to 19). Symptoms/habits that occur at this level of impairment lead to severe life limitations.

Typical symptoms at this level may include chronic self-doubt, depression and anxiety, compulsivity and obsessiveness, frequent drug or alcohol abuse, consistent failure, general shutdown of abilities, chronic and intense worry, chronic fatigue/lack of energy, physical ailments, and inability to work.

Control juggling/moderate impairment (score of 8 to 13). Symptoms/ habits that occur at this level of impairment are manageable but require monitoring.

Typical symptoms at this level may include bouts of depression, anxiety, or panic, social problems and phobias, occasional drug or alcohol abuse, chronic worry, generalized career/job dissatisfaction, mood disturbances, rigid perfectionism, fatigue, headaches, and life frustrations and agitation.

Control juggling/mild–moderate impairment (score of 2 to 7). Symptoms/habits that occur at this level of impairment represent the majority of functional problems.

Typical symptoms at this level may include social hesitations, worry, mild compulsivity and perfectionism, mild dissatisfaction with life, job frustrations, unhappiness with self, life, or relationships, and laziness.

(Note: everything to the right of Healthy Thinking on the continuum is, by degree, Reflexive Thinking.)

Follow-up

After you've been practicing working with Self-Coaching's five-step Self-Talk program for a week or two, I recommend that you replot your Reflexive Thinking tendencies. You should begin to see some major shifts toward healthy thinking. The goal of Self-Coaching is ultimately to eliminate *all* reflexive habits of control!

Personality Patterns

I'd like you to go back to chapters 3–5 and 7–10 and look up your scores from the self-quizzes you took. Using these scores along with any insightful conclusions you made, you're going to make a control pattern chart (see the following example). You will use your chart along with the visualizations from this chapter to familiarize yourself with those patterns of control that typically trip you up. How important is it for you to be able to anticipate and catch yourself *before* you short-circuit your life? Imagine you're driving a car. With awareness of your habits of control and Reflexive Thinking, it's like driving with your eyes open. Without awareness, it's like driving with your eyes closed. You decide which makes more sense.

Sample Control Pattern Chart

Name: Jane Doe
Date: June 27, 2004

1. Major personality tendencies (refer to quizzes in chapters 3–5 and 7–10):
   a. Moderate insecurity (score of 16 on chapter 3 self-quiz)
   b. Intense worrier (score of 16 on chapter 4 self-quiz)
   c. Mild control issues (score of 9 on chapter 5 self-quiz)
   d. Moderate insulator (score of 10 on chapter 7 self-quiz)
   e. Moderate compulsive-perfectionistic (score 15 on chapter 8 self-quiz)
   f. Normal deceptive tendencies (score of 3 on chapter 9 self-quiz)
   g. Mildly restricted ability to trust (score of 8 on chapter 10 self-quiz)

2. Controlling habits
   a. What-iffer
   b. Black-and-white thinker

c. Doubter
d. Should thinking
e. Have-to thinking

3. Reflexive Thinking
All tendencies fell in the mild impairment range (score in the 4 to 7 range indicating worry; mild compulsivity and perfectionism; mild dissatisfaction with life; job frustrations; unhappiness with self, life, and relationships; and laziness).

4. Summary notes
The biggest problem for me is worrying. I worry about everything. Worry has begun to cause problems at work, particularly over my performance. It seems like I'm trying too hard to be perfect and not make mistakes. Even though I'm exhausted at the end of the day, I'm having difficulty falling asleep. Mornings I wake up feeling not rested, apprehensive, insecure, and moody. My lack of desire for my husband is beginning to concern and stress me. I'm becoming a nervous wreck!

Jane Doe can now look at her chart and begin to make sense of her struggle. Her personality tendencies depict a person of moderate insecurity whose primary controlling mechanism is worrying. Since she's in the moderate range of Reflexive Thinking, she should have sufficient ability to recognize and challenge her chronic worry along with her other controlling habits. (If, however, Jane were in the moderate–severe range of Reflexive Thinking, she would have a more limited capacity to fight her tendencies. If this were the case, she would need to rely more heavily on the Self-Talk steps that follow, to develop an adequate capacity for dismantling her Reflexive Thinking).

Jane's moderate tendency toward perfectionism is probably a major contributor to her overall stress level at work. This, along with ruminative worry and performance anxiety, could readily explain why she's having difficulty falling asleep and not getting adequate rest. Jane needs to take a careful look at the shoulds and have-tos in her life; they represent her compulsive attempts to be in control by staying on top of things and not messing up. Because of her insecurity, she feels pressured to avoid any further problems by incorporating these anticipatory strategies.

Her tendency toward moderate insulation may explain her detachment from, and lack of desire for, her husband (protecting herself from rejection), and her black-and-white thinking may certainly be a reason why she does nothing to improve the relationship—the relationship is either good or bad, no in between. According to this defense: *If my relationship is bad, then why bother?* Since a tendency toward insulation also may show up in other areas (work, overall attitude toward life), Jane needs to check this out.

As you can see from this interpretation of Jane's chart, this isn't a formal calculation. You merely use the data to formulate a working picture of how control and Reflexive Thinking have contaminated your life. Keep in mind that there is no right and no wrong! Allow yourself to speculate freely. If you happen to be a bit too generous or conservative with your judgments, don't worry. In time, a process of fine-tuning will occur.

To maximize this fine-tuning effect, periodically update your chart. Retake the quizzes and reevaluate your tendencies. As you begin to learn to starve the Reflexive Thinking, thereby challenging the control habits of your life, you will notice a shifting of your scores and evaluations.

12

Step Two:
Separate Fact from Fiction

My yoga teacher, Perinkulam Ramanathan, is a very wise man. One day while preparing to sit for meditation, a beginner in the class asked, "When I meditate, my thoughts seem to run wild in my mind. How do I stop thinking?" Rama hesitated a moment, then spoke: "Your thoughts are like monkeys, always chattering and running wild. You must learn to tame your monkeys!"

If you choose to change your life, you're going to have to tame your monkeys, especially the negative, doubting, or insecure thoughts that get those monkeys chattering and screeching. Whenever you attempt to control life, you're filling your head with the chatter of insecure thinking. Monkey-running-wild thinking has many guises. Sitting up until the wee hours of the night ruminating about something you said, killing yourself to keep your house immaculate, or regretting a missed opportunity are all examples of mental monkey business.

Joyce, a forty-year-old nurse, told me about an encounter she had with a rather raucous monkey:

> I was visiting a friend on the eighth floor of the hospital. I got on the elevator, which was crowded for that time of night. I remember my first thought, *I should have taken another elevator.* All of a sudden things began to close in on me. I felt like I couldn't breathe. I felt shaky and scared. I had to get off. I wanted to

scream. I started to feel my heart pound. I started breathing faster. *What's wrong? I can't stand this. I have to get off.* My thoughts began racing. *I have to get off, I can't breathe.* I hit the alarm. Everyone looked at me blankly. I became nauseated and light-headed. I slumped on the floor of the elevator. Finally the door opened. Some of the passengers helped me out.

Now that you've established a view of your controlling habits and tendencies, it's time to begin separating your thoughts from the cacophony of screeching monkeys that have been running amok with your life. Without this separation, you become one with the monkeys. Step Two, separating fact from fiction, is the next step toward learning this indispensable technique of Self-Talk.

Jekyll or Hyde: Who's Talking?

Monkeys, Reflexive Thinking, insecurity, phew! How do thoughts—your own thoughts—run amok in your head? Does it ever feel as if there are two people living inside your head? There's your healthy, spontaneous, trusting self, and then there's your insecure, distrusting, controlling self. Which of these personalities is really you? If you want to choose a life of happiness, empowerment, and success, you must answer this question. You need to know the truth about *who* you are.

Most people are confused by the jumble of angel-devil thoughts that spin all kinds of mental mayhem: *Yes, I can. No, I can't! Maybe I could try . . . but what if I fail?* If you've been struggling, then you know that the truth is not always apparent. And if you've been struggling, then it's a given that separating fact from fiction is part of your problem.

Have you ever heard the expression "sometimes you eat the bear and sometimes the bear eats you"? For many, life is a matter of black (being the bear's meal) or white living, a vacillation of ups and downs that creates confusion. "I don't understand it, I seem so confident and in control, handling most of life's circumstances, but as soon as someone says something negative, I begin to beat myself up." What goes through your mind and, more important, what you listen to are what determine your experience of life. For example, I was working with someone who actually postponed his wedding because he was afraid to have a blood test. When I got a call from him, he was almost hysterical: "I can't go through with it. I just can't have that blood test. Am I crazy?" He wasn't crazy, but when you're caught up in reflexive, control thinking, you really do feel crazy. (It took a couple of marathon sessions, but finally the still-not-totally-convinced groom had that blood test. I just got a card from the happy couple honeymooning in the Caribbean—all is well.)

Whenever I talk about this dichotomy of separating fact (Healthy, reality-based thinking) from fiction (Reflexive, insecurity-based thinking), some people get anxious. More than once I've been asked, "Are you talking about schizophrenia?" Trust me, this isn't about schizophrenia, dual personality, or any such ominous condition. It's really not about two different personalities; there's only one personality—one you—but sometimes that you gets contaminated by insecurity. And when this happens, it can really feel like two people. So rest easy, there's only one you, one personality that's capable of two antagonistic perceptions—one healthy, and one reflexive and destructive It only *feels* like you're fragmented; you're not.

Self-Coaching Reflection
Insecurity distorts your true personality,
it doesn't change it.

It is helpful to keep this dichotomy—fact vs. fiction—in mind as you fight off the habits of insecure thinking. Look at the following examples:

I doubt that I can handle this job. Fact or fiction?
You would ask yourself, *Is it a fact that I can't handle the job?* Since you don't know whether you can handle the job unless you risk trying, you would have to conclude that this is fiction. Only if you attempted the job and failed could you say it was fact.

I'm fifty-four years old. I'll never find a boyfriend. Fact or fiction?
Of course this is fiction. It may feel like fact, but no one has a crystal

ball. Anytime you start prognosticating, no matter how statistically probable you feel a prediction may be, remember: the future is *always* an abstraction. Facts are not abstractions, they're here-and-now realities!

Did you hear how she spoke to me? Obviously she doesn't like me. Fact or fiction?

Mind reading is not factual. Like anticipating the future, it doesn't matter how "plausible" your interpretation may be; unless you verify your assumption, it remains fiction. In this example, the person may simply have been having a bad day. Nothing to do with you, just venting.

Self-Coaching Reflection
Feelings, prognostications, or attempts at mind reading
are not facts. Stop treating them as if they are.

Confusing fact with fiction is the domain of insecurity; it's where those pesky monkeys live. Since everyone has monkeys (doubts, fears, misperceptions, negativity, etc.), your choice is either to tame or to feed them. The first step in learning how to feel better and creating the life you want is learning to stop tossing bananas to those monkeys. This process begins the moment you start separating fact from fiction. Just this attempt awakens in you the realization that you have a choice. If you've been frustrated and unhappy, it's because you've been living a *choiceless*, reflexive life—no other reason. Seeing that you have a choice is big. *Very* big! This alone will immediately begin to alter your entire outlook on life. You'll see.

Look Who's Talking: Your Psychological Voice

None of the steps involved in Self-Coaching is that complicated. Neither is riding a bike—not once you learn to balance yourself. To learn balance in your life, you have to take a fresh look at your thinking. From the many people I've worked with, I'm convinced that most don't think about thinking, especially the thinking that gets them in trouble. They simply think and then react to their thoughts. John, a high school basketball player I was working with, told me, "I'm quitting the team. I can't shoot anymore." I asked him to explain what he meant by "can't." He replied, "In practice I can hit the basket from anywhere on the court, but as soon as I'm in a game, I freeze up. I can't stand the embarrassment anymore."

John isn't thinking about what he's thinking; he's simply reacting to a fear that he *can't* shoot. When John says, "I can't shoot anymore," this is, of course, fiction. The fact is, he didn't forget how to shoot (he does just fine in practice), he unfortunately is just listening to the fiction that says "I can't." His belief has become *I can't, therefore I don't.* John is a victim of his insecurity. So the question is this: rather than being controlled by fiction, how do you untangle the distortions in your mind and choose to start dealing with facts? The answer's coming; it's called Self-Talk.

John needs to recognize that his doubt isn't the truth, it's only a contaminant that's keeping him from the truth. Let me make this point very clear. If John broke his wrist and had it in a cast, then he could quite legitimately say, "I can't shoot." This would be a statement of fact. With all limbs healthy, when John says, "I can't shoot," he's simply saying, I *feel* that I can't shoot. And as you've learned, feelings are not facts. John needs to get into his head and begin separating himself from this doubt. But for now, this first step will allow John to begin to put the brakes on spinning more negatives.

❖ ❖ ❖

SELF-COACHING POWER DRILL

Your actual Self-Talk training begins now. In any struggle, conflict, or intense emotional state, distinguish whether you're responding to fact or fiction. Keep in mind that facts are verifiable, objective, and observable phenomena, while fictions are based on interpretations, judgments, and probability predictions. Once you make this distinction, *then* begin to scrutinize these thoughts. For example, tell yourself: *See, I'm allowing myself to get all worked up. I'm allowing the fiction that I'm not good enough to ruin my date!*

For now, *don't* bother changing your ways. All that's required in this drill is to call a fiction a fiction. The next time you get caught up in one of insecurity's fictions, just be willing to take it on the chin and admit it. Be patient; Step Two is only about recognizing what's going on in your inner dialogue. Step Three is where you'll actually begin challenging your destructive thinking.

Self-Fulfilling Prophecy

John's basketball disability, mentioned above, represents what we commonly call a self-fulfilling prophecy. If you treat your fictions (negatives, fears, and doubts) as facts, *they actually can become facts* (failures, lack of success, rejections). Greg, a young man in his early thirties, will make this point clear. He told me that he'd been feeling insecure and lonely. His conclusion was "I'll never find a girlfriend." Greg was telling me of a friend who had called him and, refusing to take no for an answer, convinced him to go to a party on the weekend. Greg reluctantly agreed, but had had regrets all week because of what he "knew would happen"—he was convinced he would wind up alone and depressed again.

After the party, Greg told me how he had walked in the door that night already feeling uneasy and out of place. As the night dragged on, he found himself sulking alone in a corner, drinking only with the intention of "getting a buzz." That night, after the party, lying in bed angry and depressed, Greg once again told himself that he would never meet anyone. He just wasn't lucky in love.

The prophecy—"I'll never find a girlfriend"—had been fulfilled, at least from Greg's perspective. But let's take a closer look.

Prior to the party, Greg's insecurity produced self-doubts and promises of negativity. These fictions began to steer not only his feelings, but also his behavior that night. When Greg's friend called him the next day, Greg got an earful: "You're really a piece of work. You really embarrassed me. Do you know how many people came up to me and asked, 'What's up with Greg? He looks like he wants to bite someone's head off.' The cute girl I introduced you to told me that you were attractive but unapproachable. She thought you were stuck-up."

Greg found these observations illuminating. He was finally beginning to understand what I meant when I told him that you actually become what you think. Greg's self-fulfilling prophecy demonstrates why it's so important to separate from and not identify with fiction. If you allow yourself to be swept up by insecurity, you'll wind up with exactly what you deserve—half a life, filled with uncertainty and problems. Problems that just keep repeating themselves.

Self-Coaching Reflection
You become what you think.

❖ ❖ ❖

SELF-COACHING POWER DRILL

Understanding How Your Mind Works

It's easier to explain what's going on in your mind if you think of your thoughts as if they're part of a dialogue. To help you understand this concept, I'd like you to try a little exercise. On a blank sheet of paper, write your answer to the question: "How am I feeling today?" After you've written one or two sentences, stop.

What did you learn? Perhaps you learned that you're doing okay, but you're feeling a bit rushed and compulsive about your chores. Maybe you learned that you're frustrated or angry. For the sake of this exercise, rather than looking at *what* you wrote, I'd like you to look at *how* you expressed these thoughts. For example, let's say you wrote, "I'm so unhappy. I wish there were a way for me not to be so down all the time." Who were you talking to? Obviously you were talking to yourself. But if you were talking to yourself, who was talking? And who was listening?

Rather than pursuing an elaborate philosophical or linguistic explanation for these questions, let's just say that a part of you talks and another part of you listens. Then you either accept or reject what's being said. If you accept what's being said, you become identified with it. In the above example you're telling yourself, "I'm so unhappy. . . ." If you accept this thought, you become unhappy. You identify with what you're hearing. You could, however, reject what you're hearing and fight back, saying, "What can I do to change how I feel?"

Look back at what you wrote. Can you see that it's a kind of mental talk? We do this all the time, but usually, since we're not attending to these dialogues, they go unnoticed. Of course, this isn't talking in an auditory sense; you don't actually hear these voices with your ears. It's psychological talk, an altogether normal inner dialogue I call Self-Talk. As you begin to observe your Self-Talk dialogues, you'll notice that insecurity (fiction) has its own distinct voice. This is the Reflexive Thinking voice that hurts you. Once you begin to see what's really going on, when you add awareness to what has been purely habit, you'll find that separating fact from fiction becomes almost automatic.

Separating Fact from Fiction: Doing It

If you're like most people, the habits of insecurity that contaminate your life probably operate unnoticed on a reflexive, habit level. And since most habits begin to feel natural over time, you're probably not aware of the impact they're having on your life. When, for example, people say, "I can't handle pressure" or "I'm depressed," they may know they're struggling but have no idea that they have a choice not to struggle.

There are a couple of reasons for this confusion. When you say "*I'm* depressed" or "*I* can't handle pressure," not only are you treating your symptoms of insecurity as if they are unalterable facts, but more important, you're identifying yourself with them! By saying, "*I* am depressed"—or anxious, unhappy, negative, suspicious, hyper, compulsive, and the like—in essence you're saying, "*I am* my depression."

And when you do this, there's no difference between you and your depression. As you've learned, when it comes to your psychological reality, your habits of insecurity are anything but unalterable facts of life. They're fictions that are merely being treated as facts.

Let's say you're feeling depressed. The key is to make the following distinction: "Yes, I feel depressed, but the truth is, *I'm* not depressed, a part of me is. It's just a part of me!" This simple recognition puts you in a much better position to be more objective. And with some objectivity, fact and fiction begin to become less muddled. I know it may sound like I'm playing with words, but words can change your life! And just recognizing that you have a choice can be a major awakening. How long have you been going through life feeling powerless, unable to handle situations because you were too caught up in the fiction that you and your struggle were one and the same? How often have you muttered the fiction *I can't* when faced with a life challenge?

Once you realize that there are options, you'll no longer feel trapped by life. Separating fact from fiction is the first action step toward psychological emancipation and understanding that you have a choice to choose the life you want rather than the one you feel stuck with.

Sure Sounds like a Child

There's one last concept that can be a major asset to you in your efforts to separate fact from fiction. During times when you find yourself struggling with life, if you listen carefully to your thoughts, you will invariably notice a primitive, childlike quality to them. When you see yourself whining and sulking, quitting or retreating, dreading or ruminating, you can be sure that you're being influenced not just by here-and-now reality but also by a habit that was established years ago. Your insecurity has its roots buried deep in your childhood, so its imprint on you today will be distinctly childlike.

What do I mean that thoughts have a childlike quality? Go to a mall one day and catch an earful of children whimpering about the toys they're being deprived of, screaming over being told no to an ice cream cone, crying and pouting about wanting to go home, or throwing a tantrum just because they happen to be spoiled brats. By learning to listen carefully to your thoughts, you'll see many of these same tendencies. They're all examples of the vestige of the child in you who just doesn't want to handle life—poor baby!

❖ ❖ ❖

SELF-COACHING POWER DRILL

From now on, when struggling, ask yourself, *Is what I'm hearing mature and reasonable, or does it sound disproportionate, foolish, and childlike?* Make it a point to compile a list of these childish tendencies. You'll find that these tendencies act as early warning signals for the habit that follows. By picking up your unique child voice, you will be in a position to step back and remind yourself, for example: *"My child habit wants to stamp my feet and let her have it, but what's the more mature response? Okay, deep breath, I'm going to discuss this like a grown-up."* Bottom line: you don't have to go on feeding the same habits of insecurity that have followed you around since you were a child, the same habits that reduce you to *becoming* the child you once were. Step Three is going to tell you how to stop the feeding. But first I'd like to introduce you to Jason.

Jason is a twenty-year-old student who didn't take his girlfriend Laurie's news very well. She told him that she was going to Cancún on Christmas break with a few friends. Jason wrote the following entry in his journal later that night (this is a good example of the process involved in separating Healthy from Reflexive, childlike thinking):

> I want to trust Laurie, but when she told me she was going to Cancún, I lost it. I got angry, I accused her of not loving me. I hated her! It's been a few hours and now I'm beginning to realize that when she told me she was going away, I began acting like a child who immediately concluded she was going there to cheat on me. I felt vulnerable and scared. I turned on her, I guess believing

that if I hated her, I didn't have to care what happened to her. What I need to do is force myself to recognize my "other" side [Jason's mature, uncontaminated self]. My child reflex doesn't want me to do this; he just wants to be hateful. Okay, but I can see that it's my child reflex that makes me feel threatened—not me! Laurie has never given me any reason to distrust her—never! Now I have a choice. I can believe my child reflex or call Laurie and apologize. I know what's right. It's just hard to turn off the panic.

Jason called. Laurie went to Cancún. Jason lived.

Jason's entry is an excellent example of how you will have to scrutinize your reactions to life's challenges. Whenever you're feeling trapped by insecurity, remind yourself that you have a choice.

Self-Coaching Reflection
In any conflict, if you recognize who's talking,
you'll recognize you have a choice.

13

Step Three:
Stop Listening to the Noise

Remember the old joke, "Doc, my arm hurts when I move it like this. What should I do?" To which the good doctor replies, "Stop moving it like that." If your life is hounded by negativity, doubt, or self-distrust, my advice is the same: stop thinking like that! And I'm not joking. If you want to turn your life around, you'll have to learn to stop thinking like a failure, a loser, or someone who is *almost* happy. What may surprise you is that it's really not that complicated, not with Self-Talk.

A Self-Talk Philosophy

Many people are confused about the true nature of healing, because we've been encouraged by traditional therapy, media, and self-help to become overthinkers who chronically insist on asking, *Why?* As stimulating as an exploration into the unconscious or your history may be, in my opinion, if you're looking to change—really change—it's a waste of time. Self-Coaching isn't concerned with your historical relationship to your mother or whether you were an only child, an orphan, rich, or poor. It's not *why* you started your habit of insecurity that matters, it's what you're going to do about it.

Here's how.

Self-Talk teaches you that Healthy Thinking is a choice. You've already learned how to begin separating Healthy, fact-based thinking from Reflexive, fiction-based thinking. Step Three is even more straightforward: once you figure out that Reflexive Thinking is steering your thoughts, stop listening! My grandmother used to have an expression when she'd catch me worrying about something: *You can't stop a bird from flying into your hair, but you don't have to help him build a nest!* Grandma was right; you can't stop Reflexive Thinking from popping up in your mind, but you don't have to feed and fertilize it (build a nest) with a second thought and a third and a fourth, and so on. From now on, no more nest-building.

Insecurity may speak loudly and try to convince you otherwise, but you've learned in Step Two that insecurity (those pesky monkeys) is only a part of you. There's another part of you, a healthy part, that can choose not to be deceived by these fictions. Whereas Steps One and Two are more contemplative, Step Three is definitely an action step. And the action required is to make yourself stop listening.

I have two children, and through the years I've been awakened by just about everything: sleepwalking, nightmares, nausea, and once because of an unusually large black carpenter ant that had mercilessly sunk its pincers into my son's leg! Parents have a special ear that listens for these nocturnal calls for help. What's interesting is how when anything less compelling tries to wake you up—thunder, road noise, dogs barking, alarm clocks—you have a way of resisting and falling back to sleep. But when it comes to those 911 calls from your kids, in a flash you're awake and moving toward the distress call.

Why, when the alarm goes off and you find yourself saying, "One more minute . . . just one more minute," do you feel so powerless to make yourself get out of bed? Yet when awakened from a sound sleep by a call of distress, you're able to respond immediately. Why is this? There are certain things in life you say no to and mean it. Like robbing banks or ignoring your boss's request. And there are certain things in life you say no to and don't mean it. As any child with a weak parent knows, no doesn't necessarily mean no.

Why is our ability to make healthy choices so fickle? The answer is simple: bad habits! You get used to indulging yourself—just one more taste, one more minute, one more beer—and you begin to distrust your own voice: no doesn't mean no. When it came to the habit of smoking, Mark Twain said it was the easiest habit in the world to break: "I've done it thousands of times." When your word means nothing and when you capitulate to destructive impulses, you are also convincing yourself that you *can't* handle responsibility. There's that *c* word again—*I can't, therefore I don't,* in which case you've become weak and powerless. Are you nodding your head? If you are, let me tell you it's not true. You're not weak and powerless; it only feels that way! It's all part of a deceptive habit of impotence that, given the right circumstance (like kids calling in the night), you can override with power, potency, and action. Trust me on this. The power is there, waiting for you. It doesn't have to be acquired, it only has to be accessed.

If you're like most people, initially you'll stumble trying to figure out how you can stop negative, insecure thinking, especially if it's a habit you've had for years: "I can't control what goes through my mind! It just happens." Not true. It *doesn't* just happen! Linda, a thirty-two-year-old police dispatcher, was perplexed:

> My thoughts are my biggest problems. That must be because a
> part of me is believing these thoughts. I would love to be able to
> let go of these thoughts and just say no, to somehow not identify
> with them. I woke up this morning feeling very anxious about a
> lot of stupid things. Just what am I supposed to do? I worry about
> it; as you've said, I feed it. I try to remind myself that this is just
> temporary and will pass. I tried saying no, but I can't stop the
> flood of thoughts. This childlike part of me is tricky. When I
> finally catch myself in a distortion, my reflex is quick to follow up
> with another thought, and before I realize it, I'm off running
> with another worry. I can be ten minutes into a worry cycle and
> not even realize it. Strange how my mind works.

Linda was trying not to listen, but she wasn't succeeding. Why not? It's for the same reason that you don't get out of bed when the alarm goes off: because when you tell yourself something, you don't really mean it.

SELF-COACHING POWER DRILL

Here's an experiment I'd like you to try (it worked very well for Linda). Starting right now, I want you to find an easy, not-too-stressful challenge that requires you not to listen to your typical thoughts of insecurity. For example, you might decide, "I'm not going to have my usual high-calorie snack before I go to bed tonight. I will say no!" Or perhaps, "I'm not going to procrastinate any more; I will get my bills done this morning." Once you pick your challenge, I want you to write a formal contract with yourself. For example: "I refuse to listen to my cravings. I will say no to them and not eat before going to bed." Or, "It doesn't matter what I say to distract myself, I will not listen to any thoughts that interfere with my getting those bills done before noon."

✣ ✣ ✣

There is only one goal in the above experiment: stop listening to Reflexive Thinking. And remember, no moaning or groaning! If the fate of the world depended on your not having that snack, I'm sure you'd find a way to be tough. Don't kid yourself: you *can* stop listening. But only you can decide—*must* decide—when you're ready to choose the life you want.

Try to recall the last time you decided to say no and stop listening to insecurity. How did you do it? You may have said, "No, I'm not going to do that!" And lo and behold, you did what you said—you stopped listening. Magic? Not quite. You probably called it willpower or self-discipline. Either way, you managed to say no and do what you said. It's really not complicated. All I'm asking you to do is apply this same willful approach to Reflexive Thinking.

It's a good idea to repeat the above "saying no" experiment often—you need the practice. Throw out those old hesitations and start getting used to the fact that you really can say no. With continued practice you'll begin to build solid psychological muscle that will enable you to become tough as nails with any and all unruly childish tantrums.

Self-Coaching Reflection
If you think you can't say no and mean it, you're wrong.

Using Your Imagination

Before leaving this section, I want to share one last, extremely important technique. I've found that when it comes to saying no to Reflexive Thinking, creating the right mental image can make all the
difference. I strongly suggest that you find and employ an image that
works for you. You can be creative and form your own image, or try
one from the following list:

Shutting the watertight doors
If you've ever been on a military ship or seen movies of submarines,
you've probably noticed the large watertight doors between compart-
ments. These doors are meant to be closed should there be damage to
the hull. Insecurity is like water that tries to leak through a partially
closed door. What begins as a trickle of worry or doubt can, in time,
turn into a torrent that floods you with anxiety, panic, or excess emotion. Every time you catch yourself listening to Reflexive Thinking, see
yourself slamming shut the steel door, turning the lock, and stopping
the leak. Once you seal your watertight door, Reflexive Thoughts can't
affect you.

Kicking the soccer ball
Imagine yourself on a large soccer field. Your job is to keep the field free
of stray soccer balls from neighboring fields. As you walk along, a soccer ball rolls by. You approach it and *whack*—you kick it off the field.
Reflexive Thoughts can be seen as soccer balls infiltrating your conscious field of view. When one comes in, kick it out . . . another *whack!*
At first there will be many balls converging on your field, but as long
as you see yourself aggressively clearing your field, the frequency will
quickly diminish.

Body punching
In boxing the objective is to defeat your opponent. Most of the time
this is accomplished not with a single knockout punch, but with a

series of body punches that eventually weaken your opponent to the point where one punch will finish him off. Reflexive Thinking is your opponent, and unless you're lucky, one punch won't knock it out of your life. Instead, begin to imagine that every time you say no to Reflexive Thinking, you're throwing a body punch. Turn away from doubt—body punch! Take a risk—body punch!

Disciplining the child

Since there is a distinct primitive quality to Reflexive Thinking, it's not hard to hear—and imagine—a whiny, tantrumy, childlike quality to these thoughts. What would you do if you were in charge of a spoiled, bratty child? I hope you'd take charge and set this child straight: "Now, cut that out! Enough of your carrying on!" With an out-of-control, manipulative child you need to be strong; consistent; and, most important, clear in your approach. "I said no!" Remember, you're in charge, not the child.

Letting go of the balloons

If you find the above images a bit too aggressive, you may like something more serene. Imagine Reflexive Thoughts as helium-filled balloons that you hold in your hands. When you find yourself intimidated by insecurity, just open your hands, let go of the strings, and sit back as you watch the balloons drift off into the sky—smaller and smaller until they finally vanish.

14

Step Four: Let Go

At this point in your reading, you've learned to isolate your controlling tendencies, you know how to separate fact from fiction, and you're working on saying no to Reflexive Thinking. Now, with Step Four, we're going for the prize—you're going to eliminate struggle from your life! What I'm going to suggest may sound almost contradictory to what you've been doing until now because for the first time you're not going to be *thinking* about what to do, at least not in the formal sense. And what's the opposite of thinking? Learning to *let go* of thoughts. Self-Talk was necessary to bring you to this level—you needed to *separate* and see what was going on, then you needed to *stop* the avalanche of insecurity, and now you're in a position to finally let it go—*it* being struggle, insecurity, and Reflexive Thinking. From now on your mantra will be: *separate, stop, and let go.*

Tubing: Your Stream of Consciousness

My nieces Chrissy and Kathy (my not-so-identical twins from chapter 3) are from the Woodstock area of New York State. One summer they convinced us to join them in something I had never heard of before: tubing. As the name implies, tubing consists of floating down a fast-moving stream in a giant inner tube. The tube itself is outfitted with a board strapped in the center of the doughnut hole, referred to as the "butt board," which promises to spare your bottom from the many jagged boulders along the way. Surely, I thought, this wouldn't be necessary. I found out differently: tubing is quite an experience, one that can be rather deceptive at first. Once you're in the icy mountain water, the current quickly grabs hold of your tube, at which point you are one with the stream—and the boulders and the swirling eddies. Thank God for the butt board.

Thoughts of insecurity race through our minds like a rushing stream. Not a stream of water, but one of consciousness—a stream of anxiety consciousness (pun intended). When you're caught in a current of insecurity, instead of boulders, you crash into fears, doubts, and hesitations about your life. And when you're bobbing along this stream of insecure, Reflexive Thinking, you probably don't notice that you're drifting toward more treacherous currents, which can swiftly carry you into habits of hopelessness, anxiety, stress, or even depression. Once you're swept along, the stream dictates the course of your life, and it can seem impossible to stop.

When I was in my tube that day, racing downstream at a very respectable clip, had it not been for a collision with a boulder in the center of the stream, I would have missed one simple truth. After pulling myself out of the icy water, I saw that I was in water only up to my waist! I could have stepped out of my tube at any time. When you're bobbing along your stream of insecurity consciousness, it may not occur to you either that the solution may be simple. And safe.

Remember that your stream of insecurity gives you the impression that you're powerless. But it's *only* an impression! All you need to do is learn how to get out of the stream. To do this, you're going to have to get out of your tube and get a little wet. Steps One, Two, and Three have prepared you for this disembarkation, and now it's time to get out of the stream of insecurity and start living differently. Insecurity has long ago convinced you that everything near and dear depends on controlling life, but now you know better. Now you can find out the truth, that your stream is only waist deep!

Less Is More

Most overthinkers or control types have no problem with Steps One, Two, or Three because these are *thinking* steps. This is where you live, in your head, and of course you feel safe as long as you're just thinking about life. Now you need to be challenged in a way you're not used to—by *not* thinking. By letting go. This is why I said that to get out of your stream of insecurity consciousness, you're going to have to get wet. Getting out of your tube may feel a bit uncomfortable and unfamiliar, but to get to the shore (and out of your stream of Reflexive Thinking) there's no other way. Trust me, it won't hurt you.

"Stop thinking?" You're probably thinking I'm crazy. You've been spinning out thoughts at such a rate for so many years that the notion of stopping your thoughts may seem impossible. It's not. And keep in mind that we're not trying to stop *all* thoughts, just the insecurity-driven ones. Before discussing the specifics of how to stop insecurity thinking, let me tell you what originally convinced me that thinking wasn't the answer.

Wanted: Joe Luciani

My wife and I had just gotten married and I was returning home from work one day to be greeted by a registered letter from the court system in Queens, New York. The letter informed me that a warrant had been issued for my arrest! It went on to state that my wife, a woman named Rosa, had filed charges asserting that I had been delinquent on my child support payments for the past two years!

Panicky thoughts of spending the night somewhere in a Queens jail began to fill my consciousness. I called my friend Alex, an old roommate and lawyer who assured me there was nothing to worry about (easy for him to say) and that he would take care of things. A few long moments passed and he called back saying that, unfortunately, it wasn't going to be that easy. He would have to go to the courthouse in the morning.

That night I imagined one complication after another. I was help-lessly watching my molehills growing into a mountain range. I felt myself getting physically upset over all the what-ifs. I knew rationally that this would all be straightened out one day, but it was getting to *that day* that had me in a tailspin. I'll admit, most of my worries were far-fetched and far from rational. (If you've seen the movie *Midnight Express,* I was imagining scenarios reminiscent of the barbaric Turkish prison in the movie.)

While in the throes of this emotional, chaotic frenzy, a bubble of sol-ace somehow reached my consciousness. An altogether simple truth emerged among the deluge of chaotic what-iffing. *Everything in my life—one way or another—has been resolved.* I know this sounds rather simplistic, but it was truly an "ah-ha" revelation that night. There had been countless challenges in my life—some big, many small—but each and every one of them had passed, gotten resolved, or ceased to affect me.

The next morning Alex called back. Sure enough, it was a computer problem that was resolved. I came away from that needlessly harrow-ing experience feeling altogether ridiculous for being so hysterical, but more important, I took with me the understanding that with anxiety, less is definitely more! I realized that everything that was hurting me was because of my intense thinking. The question *What if I didn't have those thoughts?* occurred to me. Do you know what the answer was? Had I not had those thoughts, I would have been fine. Sure I would have been concerned, but I would have trusted the statistical truth of my life (the previous facts of my life) and realized that one way or another, things get resolved, settled, or eliminated. I would have slept better, been less anxious, and escaped a few gray hairs. If only I could have stopped those worry thoughts!

Sure, you're only trying to be prepared for the worst, yada yada yada, but does worry or any other thoughts of control do anything to *really* prepare you? Of course not. Your instinctual reactions are far more effective than any rehearsed or concocted strategy. And some-times—if you're willing to risk trusting your four-million-plus years of instinctual and intuitional heritage—doing absolutely nothing, just sitting back, letting go, and letting life unfold as you collect more data, is the simplest, most effective thing you can do. And sometimes, as in my deadbeat-dad debacle, it's the *only* really worthwhile thing to do.

Three Ways to Let Go

There are three methods for learning to let go. What method works best for you depends on your unique circumstances and personality. It certainly wouldn't hurt to employ all three methods, which I heartily recommend. The three methods are Changing the Channel, Therapeutic Recklessness, and Meditation. Let's start with the simplest, Changing the Channel.

Changing the Channel

When I drive, I like to listen to classical music. I was driving home from my yoga class yesterday, feeling completely serene, listening to Mozart, and enjoying the snow-covered vista. My drift into a mellow reverie was disrupted by the shrill voice of an announcer hawking replacement windows for a one-time-only, low, low, low price! Serenity beginning to slip, I reached for the channel selector on my radio and switched to a light jazz station. Ah, back to the snow, the calm, the reverie. That was easy.

When you're listening to radio, it comes naturally to demand what pleases you. You just Change Channels. Keep this simple metaphor in mind as you find yourself listening to insecurity's shrill voice trying to sell you a life of negativity, doubt, and fear. Next time you find your serenity interrupted, imagine yourself taking another action step—Changing the Channel. Here's a simple exercise to help you see how easy this can be.

❖ ❖ ❖

SELF-COACHING POWER DRILL

Think about something negative that happened to you (an embarrassing moment, a frightening experience, etc.). Next, think about something emotionally positive—a memory, an aspiration, or a vision for the future—anything that evokes good feelings. On one side of a blank sheet of paper write down the negative experience; on the other side write down the positive experience.

Now, for approximately thirty seconds, look at the negative statement and allow yourself to think only about this thought—nothing else. Think anything you want, as long as it focuses on the negativity of this experience. At the end of thirty seconds, turn the page over and *force yourself* to think only about the positive experience. At first this may take a little practice and patience.

Once you get the hang of switching from negative to positive, try this: Start by looking at the negative statement and allowing negatives to fill your mind. Then at any point, impulsively flip the page and switch to positive thinking. As you progress with this exercise you will find that at any point, negatives can be stopped and flipped into positives.

The above exercise is designed to convince you that at any point you can Change Channels and stop listening to destructive, insecure Reflexive Thinking. Once you realize how easy Changing the Channel can be, you'll understand the true meaning of the word *empowerment*. And the good news is that it's no harder than pressing the selector button on your radio. Don't like what you're hearing? Turn it off!

Snowblower Blues

This past year, New Jersey got walloped with an early winter snowstorm. Henry was so excited about not listening to his Reflexive Thinking and Changing the Channel, he couldn't wait to tell me the news:

> Last night I went out to try my new snowblower. Two minutes into blowing the snow, the machine stopped—dead! After a few hours of trying to figure out what was wrong, I gave up and went into the house. I sat down and was feeling completely bummed out, tired, and frustrated. How was I going to find someone to repair the machine? Who could I call? How in the world would I be able to transport this monster?

I noticed that I was getting swallowed up in a foul, worrisome mood. Mostly I was feeling like my life was fragmented. Something was broken and I couldn't fix it. But what was worse was my childlike reflex, guilting me, telling me I had wasted my money (my wife still reminds me) and never should have bought the stupid thing. If I had let my Reflexive Thinking continue, I guarantee I would have begun to panic. It sounds like I'm exaggerating, but I'm not—I was really getting worked up.

Thank God I remembered our talk about Changing the Channel. I needed to find that selector button in my brain so I could stop this nonsense and just let it go. I sat down, poured a cup of coffee, and told myself: *I don't know how I'm going to fix the damn thing, but I always manage to figure things out. I'm going to let go of all this whining now and trust that, come tomorrow, I'll find the answers I need. I'll give my brother a call; I'm sure he can't wait to tell me how warm it is in Florida—that will Change my Channel.* Even though my mind wanted to go on yapping about how terrible my situation was, I decided that I wasn't going to go on feeling crummy. No way! *Click*—I switched the channel.

Sure enough, after about ten minutes talking to my brother, I had completely forgotten about the snowblower. Well, I didn't completely forget about it, but I was able to let it go and go take a well-deserved hot bath.

Once Henry stopped listening to Reflexive Thinking and decided to Change the Channel, he began to figure things out and gain some much-needed perspective. And why wouldn't he? Henry, like you, has handled countless life challenges before. Why not this one? Why indeed? We certainly have the ability to handle life, but when contaminated by reflexive insecurity, truth means nothing. The truth can mean something, can change your life, only if you stop your Reflexive Thinking and start dealing with fact rather than fiction. Changing the Channel is a way to break the stranglehold of spiraling thoughts that are doing nothing for you except, as Henry would tell you, bumming you out.

Therapeutic Recklessness

Insecurity and control lead to a bottled-up kind of life, leaving you vigilant, always looking over your shoulder and expecting trouble. You've become an overthinker. When challenged by life, you find yourself becoming leery, rigid, overly cautious, inhibited, fearful, and distrusting of self and of life. If you struggle, I don't have to tell you about the congestion you feel when your thoughts become contaminated with Reflexive Thinking.

Oftentimes, when working with control-sensitive people, if I mention my concept of letting go, I'm met with stern resistance: *You must be joking. I can't let it go. How can I forget what he said to me? What if I run into him on the street? What if he tells his friends? What if . . . ?* The problem is that letting go of insecurity feels downright dangerous. If you recall, one of the fundamental tenets of Self-Coaching states that controlling life is a myth. When caught up in Reflexive Thinking, you're also caught up in the myth that your efforts are protecting you from life. Letting go, not worrying, trusting—these may sound like sensible ideas, but they seem much too risky.

✤ ✤ ✤

SELF-COACHING POWER DRILL

Pep Talks

When I first began to develop Self-Coaching I relied heavily on what I called Pep Talks. I found that with ongoing encouragement, I could eventually get people to take the plunge and risk trusting life. In fact, I still encourage this practice and strongly recommend you try it. Just imagine yourself as the coach walking through the locker room. The insecure, fearful, unhappy, controlling part of you is the athlete who's feeling altogether listless and defeated. But remember, you're the coach. You know the energy's being sopped up by a spiral of negativity, and you need to stop it!

What would a coach say? For one thing, a coach doesn't accept negativity or defeat. A coach overrides these obstacles by lighting a fire, by inciting the will to overcome, to win, to succeed. A good coach will do everything necessary: ranting, raging, encouraging, stimulating, challenging, whatever it takes. The next time you find yourself slumping, Pep Talk the part of you that's giving up. Start raising the roof. Don't accept powerlessness or excuses; only accept a willingness to overcome any and all adversity. The difference between success and failure is all attitude.

Although my Pep Talks always seemed to have beneficial results, I was looking for something more, a kind of hook—something that would act more as a focus of understanding as well as a motivation for change. A Pep Talk with a hook was what I needed.

Samantha, a twenty-five-year-old florist, gave me the insight I needed:

> I think I need to watch my drinking. When I go out with the girls, I find I need a few drinks to loosen up. Then a few more. I don't get drunk or anything, but you wouldn't believe the transformation I go through. It's as if someone pumped me up with confidence. It's unbelievable. I don't worry or care about anything, I'm willing to talk to strangers, I feel good about myself. I can see why people turn into alcoholics.

I had heard this many times from many people; the profound effects of alcohol clearly can be quite seductive for someone bottled up with insecurity and life hesitations. A psychiatrist I interned with often referred to alcohol as the best anti-anxiety drug available (which is why it can be so dangerous). What does alcohol do psychologically? For starters, it builds a false sense of confidence while simultaneously loosening inhibitions. With fewer fears and doubts, someone drinking is more likely to be impulsive. This is the primary danger in drinking: heightened false confidence with a grandiose sense of competence.

Combine this with a not-caring attitude, impaired judgment, and diminished physical ability, and, as you well know, alcohol can be a very destructive drug indeed.

In spite of the obvious reasons for not wanting to encourage Samantha to keep drinking, I did want her to notice what happened when she was intoxicated. I asked her to notice how everything in her world changed when she didn't care about her insecurity. The point was well taken, and Samantha and I began to work on what we called having a psychological cocktail.

Not wanting to use alcohol as a positive metaphor, I began to distill (no pun intended) the essence of our little insight and came up with the fact that drinking induces a not-caring, the-hell-with-everything attitude of recklessness. And this turned out to be the hook I was looking for to teach overthinking, controlling people to let go. I call it Therapeutic Recklessness.

Let me put forth this disclaimer. There are two kinds of recklessness: destructive recklessness and Therapeutic Recklessness. Destructive recklessness has to do with impulsivity and acting out (getting into fights, stealing money, getting drunk). Therapeutic Recklessness has everything to do with letting go of insecurity-driven control—nothing else. Maybe Therapeutic Recklessness doesn't sound so reckless to you, but if you reflect a moment and recall times where you were worrying, doubting, or fearfully anticipating some future event, you know how hard it is to let go. Remember my night worrying about going to the Queens jail? Without your usual controlling juggle, you may feel uncomfortable or in danger. The concept of "me without my control" may feel altogether alien and threatening, yet this is exactly when you most need a psychological cocktail called recklessness: *The heck with it! I'm just not going to worry about what she thinks.* Or, *He didn't like what I said? What can I say? I'm not going to lose sleep over it!*

Let's go back to Samantha and her alcohol experience. If you recall, alcohol allowed her "not to care" as much about her usual concerns. It's important to understand that *caring* isn't Samantha's problem (nor is caring about life your problem). It's only when caring is driven to excess by insecurity and Reflexive Thinking that you find yourself *caring much too much!* Letting go isn't about *not* caring, or not being concerned (remember our discussion in chapter 4 about concern vs. worrying: concern deals with fact, worry with fiction), it's about not caring so much. Here are some simple exercises that might help you get the idea:

1. When it comes to self-trust, tell yourself *I'm going to be reckless—and believe that I'll be okay.*

2. Give yourself a little Pep Talk and fire yourself up enough to be willing to risk letting go of your typical controlling strategies. *Go for it!*

3. Imagine yourself taking a psychological cocktail and becoming drunk with confidence.

4. Realize that overthinking is your problem. Become reckless by getting more involved in what you're doing and just let go of the thinking. Get lost in what you're doing, not what you're thinking.

5. Realize that any departure from your control comfort zone is going to feel reckless; don't be fooled. It's not being reckless, it's just stepping out of the box called control. It might *feel* reckless, but if you take the shot, you might be pleasantly surprised—it might begin to feel liberating!

Self-Coaching Reflection
Be willing to pursue a reckless attitude of trust.

Meditation: The Quintessential Form of Letting Go

When I first began to practice meditation, I was instructed to simply follow my breath. Nothing else; just follow my breath, in and out. It sounded so easy, until I tried. At first it seemed that every few seconds I found myself wrestling with intrusive thoughts. In time and with patience, I began to get better at keeping my focus on the breathing.

Eventually I was able to go for longer and longer periods with my total attention on my breath. As my attention grew, I found that the distracting thoughts began to recede.

Once I reached this level of meditation, the benefits became obvious. After meditating, it was as if I had been on vacation. Not only did my mind seem clearer and more alert, but also I felt completely relaxed and restored physically. This impressed me, as I left each class with a different perspective and an untroubled mind. I became curious. What was the mechanism that allowed these profound changes to take place? What was I doing when I meditated? After giving this considerable thought, I concluded that by focusing on my breath and gently letting go of distracting thoughts, I was learning how to step out of—to let go of—my normal ego consciousness, the place where worry, concern, troubles, and demands lurked. Thus, without the hounds of worldly woes nipping at my heels, I was able to release my mind and body from all the ill effects—psychological as well as physiological—that these thoughts trigger.

It occurred to me that if, through meditation, I could learn to disengage from normal consciousness, then why couldn't I apply what I learned to letting go of Reflexive Thinking? I tried it out, and it worked. If I had a worry or a fear, for example, I just cleared my mind, followed a few breaths, and was able to simply, without struggle, let these thoughts go. If I hadn't practiced and experienced this letting go in meditation, I doubt whether it would have been so simple. That's why I want to include the practice of meditation as part of your Step Four training. Meditation can teach you that Reflexive Thinking cannot rule or ruin your life—not once you let go.

I realize that not everyone is inclined to practice meditation; this need not be a cause for concern. Therapeutic Recklessness and Changing the Channel, when practiced regularly, are sufficient techniques for developing an understanding of and a capacity for letting go. Since the practice of meditation can acquaint you with a firsthand experience of liberation from thoughts, I urge you to try it, even if you don't do it regularly.

❖ ❖ ❖

SELF-COACHING POWER DRILL

Meditation: Learning to Be Still

I would describe meditation as nothing more—and nothing less—than the practice of learning to be still. If you're driven by Reflexive Thinking, learning to be still is just the ticket for proving that thoughts don't own you. Here is a simple, no-frills way to incorporate meditation into your daily life. And for our purposes of learning to let go, the good news is that a few minutes a day is all that's needed to get the point about how easy it is to let go.

First rule: don't overdo it! If you try too hard, you'll become frustrated and wind up abandoning meditation. So start out slowly. If you begin to feel too frustrated or uncomfortable, stop. From the beginning, your experience needs to be positive and restorative, certainly not painful. To experience the concept of letting go, just a minute or two at first will suffice. In time, if you want to explore the boundless benefits of meditation, you can build up to fifteen minutes, a half hour, or longer. But I must warn you: if you approach meditation with a typically Western attitude of "no pain, no gain," you will be defeating the purpose and potential benefit.

Next, find a comfortable sitting position on the floor; inserting a cushion under your tailbone can help. Crossed legs is best, but it may take some practice to sustain this position. If you sit in a chair, make sure your back is well supported, and keep your head balanced over your torso to prevent your head from drooping. As you find a comfortable position, you can either close your eyes or find a point of focus—for example, a candle or specific reference point. If you choose a candle, I find it helps to almost completely shut your eyes, just leaving a slit for the candle rays to be noticed. Try not to blink. If you feel a need to blink, just close your eyes and continue. In time you will be able to stare for longer periods of time.

Now bring your awareness to your breathing. For thousands of years the practice of meditation has centered on the breath.

Breathing acts as a hook for you to maintain a steady focus while trying to step apart from distracting thoughts. Breathe normally through your nose. It helps to experiment a bit until you can create a slight hissing sound deep in your nasal passages as you breathe in and out through the nostrils.

Many people incorporate a mantra to assist in maintaining focus. A mantra is any word or phrase that you repeat over and over with each breath. It could have personal or religious significance or, for that matter, it could be any word that appeals to you. Recapping: breathe in through the nose, aware of a slight hissing. As you inhale, you form the mantra in your mind. Exhale, silently repeat your mantra . . . inhale . . . exhale.

Here's the key: as you settle into your breathing and mantra, there is only one objective, to focus exclusively on your breath. You breathe in and you breathe out. Nothing else. This sounds easy, but trust me, it will take practice. At first you'll be hounded by one distracting thought after another. This is perfectly normal, and you shouldn't become frustrated. Just try not to follow these thoughts—let them float by without attaching to them. Let them go. Gently grab hold of your mind and bring it back to your breathing . . . in and out. Always come back to your breath.

Some people find that they need more structure. If you find these instructions too vague, you may want to try counting your breaths (each inhalation-exhalation cycle counts as one). You can start at twenty and count backward to one. If you feel you need a bit more challenge to keep you interested, try this: starting with the number one, you begin to count. Every time you have a distracting thought, go back to one. For example, let's say I breathe in and out three times without a distracting thought. On my fourth cycle I find myself thinking, *I have to remember to call Sally when I'm done.* Since I had a distracting thought, I go back to one and start counting again. At first it's not uncommon to go only two or three cycles without a distracting thought. In time you'll be able to see the improvement as you count higher and higher. Although I find this last technique a bit too competitive and frustrating for me, many report that they enjoy the challenge. See what suits you.

It's important to realize that your mind isn't accustomed to not thinking. You'll struggle at first, but *do not* be critical of these early efforts! Embrace every attempt, even if it's only for a few minutes. In time you'll find that you can follow your breath longer and longer. Eventually you'll have the unexpected experience of finding out that you can exist alongside of your normal, conscious thinking. Whereas you once felt completely identified with what went through your head, now you begin to understand that thinking is only one river that flows through you. When you step out of that river, you'll have the totally liberating experience of not being identified with your thoughts. You're still you; you're just not defining yourself by what you're thinking. In a sense, you're the you beyond your thoughts.

If you've been victimized by Reflexive Thinking, I can't stress how important it is for you to learn and have this experience of letting go. Meditation, more than any other experience, will make it very clear that you always have a choice—any thought driven by insecurity, however compulsive, demanding, or obsessive, remains an option. When you fully embrace the notion that thoughts, especially Reflexive Thinking, can simply be let go, you'll be well on your way toward personal liberation.

Finally, don't approach meditation as a tool to figure out your life or see it as a goal to be obtained. There is only one objective: being with your breath, learning to be still.

❖ ❖ ❖

SELF-COACHING POWER DRILL

The Serenity Mantra: Three Great Reasons for Letting Go

Whenever you're confronted with a problem, concern, or worry and need to let go, repeat these three simple truths. They will put you in the right frame of mind for any of the above letting-go techniques. I suggest you write them down on the back of a business card. Whenever you find your mind spinning with Reflexive Thinking, read the truths. If necessary, read them over and over again—mantralike.

1. *Let life unfold. There are obstacles but no dead ends.*
   Sometimes, when you're walloped by life, you may feel that there are no answers to life's difficulties. Rather than dead ends, perhaps a more apt perception would be *bottlenecks*. Because of Reflexive Thinking, you may find yourself constricted or bogged down—but not dead-ended. What feels to be hopeless is only a distortion of insecurity. As mentioned before, insecurity can own you if it can convince you things are hopeless.

2. *I trust that my instincts and intuition will serve me.*
   When the path is unknown or murky and you find yourself bogged down, it's time for a risk. It may be hard to convince yourself to risk trusting yourself and life, but if you're willing, take the shot and *let go, let life.* Things can happen, shift, and change, but only if you stop your bottleneck thinking.

3. *Every problem has a solution, and sometimes I have to wait for an answer.*
   Part of risking is the rational understanding that every problem has a solution. You have to be disciplined enough to tell yourself that you may have to wait for it. Insecurity, if anything, is impatient. As your anxiety or panic grows, you become more insistent on demanding an answer—now! Just because you don't know or can't see the answer doesn't mean it doesn't exist . . . only that it's beyond your view. With a willingness to trust, you put yourself in the best possible position to create the life you want.

❖ ❖ ❖

15

Step Five:
Motivate Yourself

I remember going to my daughter's fifth-grade field day competition. The last event of the day was the perennial tug-of-war. Both groups lined up on either side, a yellow flag tied to the middle of a long rope. As the bullhorn sounded, the Red team dug in their heels, as did the Blue team. The tug was on. For the longest time nothing happened; the yellow flag remained motionless as red cheeks and perspiration became the norm. Finally there was movement. An inch at first, then another. The Red team slowly, consistently, began to prevail. It looked bad for Blue.

But then it happened: a Red team member slipped, and the yellow flag was pulled about a foot toward the Blue team! Then another foot, and another. Once this movement got translated along the rope, alarm began to infect the Red team, which suddenly began to unravel as their contorted faces reflected panic. It was a sudden capitulation, as if their collective arms had turned to Jell-O, at which point the Red team was literally dragged across the line to defeat. How can we explain the Red team's complete collapse?

Understanding the dynamics of the above tug-of-war requires that we not only recognize the total collapse of the Red team but also notice what happened to the Blue team. When that fateful Red team slip was felt by the struggling Blue team, something shifted. In that moment, every Blue team child had a hint, a taste of victory. Empowered by this realization, the Blue team found renewed strength and determination. It was as if the Blue team were feasting on the energy the Red team was giving up. And once the Blue team surged with momentum, their success was assured.

Whether it's a tug-of-war or life, it's all the same mechanism. If you sense you're losing ground, whether on your job, in your relationships, or in your ability, your tendency is to feel you're losing your emotional grip—to give up. At this point you can begin to stumble with doubt and habits of insecurity. Controlling strategies become your last-ditch effort to stave off further erosion. And always, you're one step away from admitting *What's the use?* At this point you're being pulled, not by a rope, but by Reflexive Thinking.

If you've been struggling, then you've been a member of the Red team for too long. Now you're ready to join the Blue team. How? By changing your attitudes. Step Five completes your Self-Talk training, making you ready to grab on to life's rope and start tugging. But first there are two vital components that represent what might be called Self-Talk's follow-through. These components are motivation and momentum.

Follow-through

If you've played any sport—whether it's golf, tennis, baseball, or bowling—you probably know about the importance of follow-through. Hitting or throwing the ball is critically important, but unless you continue with the motion after you've released the ball, you'll never excel. This continued motion is called follow-through. Self-Talk requires follow-through if you expect to excel in creating the life you want.

Self-Talk's follow-through can be defined as what you need to do *after* you've successfully disengaged from insecurity. This is the realm of motivation and momentum. Follow-through needs to be seen not as a separate part of your Self-Talk efforts, but as an integral component of them. Combined with the first four steps of Self-Talk, learning to follow through will take you forward into a life you choose, rather than one handed to you by insecurity.

Motivation and Momentum: The Formula for Success

The first four steps of Self-Talk taught you to identify faulty, insecure thinking, then to separate fact from fiction. Then you learned to stop the runaway train of Reflexive Thinking, and finally you learned to just let it go. And if it weren't for the fact that we're dealing with entrenched, long-standing habits of insecurity, you could stop your training at this point. But as you well know, habits don't roll over and die because we challenge them. What's necessary is to challenge a habit over time, because in time, all habits will wilt and crumble. It's only a matter of time. And that's where motivation and momentum come in.

Think of motivation and momentum as first cousins. To sustain your efforts over time, you're going to need to maintain two things: the right attitude and sufficient energy. Momentum, as you're about to learn, has more to do with the energy component; motivation, more the attitude component. The equation looks like this:

$$\text{Self-Talk} + \text{motivation (the right attitude) and momentum}$$
$$\text{(sufficient energy)} + \text{time} = \text{success}$$

Momentum

There is a phenomenon that has baffled sports enthusiasts and coaches for years. A team can be losing, getting blown away, and then, just when all seems lost, something inexplicable happens that turns the tide of battle from black to white, David defeats Goliath, and in a northern New Jersey suburb, the Blue team turns it around and kills the Red team. This inexplicable something is an energy called momentum.

I've found that Self-Coaching success can be ensured if you can harness momentum. The dictionary defines momentum as the strength of force gained by motion. For our purposes I'll define momentum as the surge in energy and enthusiasm (force) you feel after a success (motion—i.e., change). If you've ever dieted, you know the surge of enthusiasm, determination, and energy you feel when you step on that scale and you've lost three pounds. Or when you go to the gym and after three weeks you notice a distinct tightening of your stomach muscles. Prior to getting encouraging results, you may find yourself plodding along, doing what you need to do, in a less enthusiastic, more mechanical fashion. But once you get results, once you feel the power and force of momentum, you begin to fly. And this is why it's critically important to have some early success to build on.

The key to launching your Self-Coaching success is to have some early victories. And for this you need to begin at the beginning, looking for small, less risky challenges. Jennifer, a thirty-three-year-old freelance editor, and I talked about gaining a bit of momentum. Armed with a thorough understanding of Self-Coaching's first four steps, Jennifer and I tried to pinpoint where she needed to experience some success. I asked her to talk about what specifically she wanted to change in her life. She responded: "Well, I guess I'd start with my marriage. Larry is totally out of control and has become verbally abusive lately. Yes, that's where I would start."

I told her that to stand up to Larry, she was going to need to need to build up some momentum and confidence. (Confidence, incidentally, is a by-product of momentum. As you feel the force of momentum, so, too, does your experience of confidence grow.) Since Jennifer was profoundly insecure and prone to doubting every choice she made, the wiser choice would be to build on a few successful experiences before challenging Larry. I suggested that we first look at her doubting tendencies. "We've talked about how insecure you feel, how you're always putting yourself down and doubting any decision you make. I'd like you to focus on one goal for this week: practice not feeding your insecurity." Jennifer recognized the practicality of her homework assignment and agreed.

A week later a very animated Jennifer told me, "I did it! I actually did it! I've been stopping my insecurity all week. Just letting it go. I'm actually getting quite good at it. The other day I was confronted by a neighbor who rudely told me she didn't like the color of my new car. A few weeks ago, I would have been distraught wondering if I made a mistake. I would have made myself crazy. This time all I did was grab hold of myself and insist: *This is just my insecurity. I am not going to feed it!* That was only one example; there were many this week. I was being quite reckless, if I say so myself." Jennifer was surging with energy.

Jennifer was pumped up. She had turned the corner and now had momentum. From this point on, it was easy. Her confidence in her

Self-Coaching was unshakable. She began with small, incremental steps (not feeding insecurity, refusing to battle her husband, risking telling the truth, etc.), but once she got up a full head of steam, she was off to much bigger skirmishes. She signed up for night classes and finally decided to pursue her displaced ambition to become an English teacher. Then she took on Larry. Last I heard, she and Larry were in couples counseling and doing very well. Jennifer's momentum and energy carried her right to the life she always wanted.

Begin with Simple Successes
Momentum will build confidence in your new abilities and your new self. Keep in mind that the first few steps, no matter how small, may still seem frightening. Remember, without control, you're going to feel like a frightened, novice skier on your first run down the mountain. But as any skier will tell you, once you learn to string together a series of zigzag traverses, any mountain can be reduced to a manageable challenge. The same goes for whatever you're struggling with. As long as you break things down into a series of practical steps, you'll be able to reduce any problem to manageable proportions.

Even though you now *know* there's no danger, you still need to take those first few steps before you will be convinced of what you know. And this does take a bit of courage. It's a leap of faith, and that's why it's helpful to connect with some of momentum's energy to fortify and carry you through. Understand, your goal isn't to win a few battles, it's to sustain you and your efforts over time until that final victory—your life—belongs to you. Not to insecurity.

This brings us back to an important point mentioned above: time. Never forget that the habits of insecurity that have been ruining your life have probably been around most of your life. Clearly, these are habits that are going to be resistant to your efforts. With incremental successes you begin to become a formidable opponent to the inertia of habit. And when the time is ripe, when the old Red team slips, that's when you tug on that rope and bring it on home. It's all about momentum. Momentum and a few positives.

Motivation: It's More than Positive Thinking

When most people first encounter Self-Talk, they tend to confuse it with "positive thinking." It's not uncommon for someone to come up to me after one of my lectures saying, "I've tried positive thinking and it didn't work." I try to assure them that even though Self-Talk replaces faulty thinking with a more empowered, truth-based thinking, it's much more than positive thinking. Positive thinking is only half the battle. The other half is positively believing.

Just telling yourself positives isn't enough, even if the positives are factual; you also have to find a way to believe them. I often hear, "I tell myself I'm smart. I'm talented. I recognize that I usually get the job done. Why do I still feel insecure?" If you want to change your life, positive thinking is just not enough. That's why so many motivational programs and self-help books wind up being disappointments. Remember, as powerful as words are, they can't and won't change you, not unless you believe them. I found this out a few years ago.

Four Hours That Changed My Life

November 6, 1988, was a dark and drizzly day in Manhattan. On that dreary morning I was one of twenty-seven thousand runners lining up to run in the New York Marathon. It was a grand, snapshot moment as fireboats in the Hudson River spewed plumes of red, white, and blue water high into the air, and TV helicopters hovered overhead with egg-beater cadence, while the claustrophobic blanket of twenty-seven thousand bodies from more than ninety countries began to come alive with energy and excitement. It was an electrifying experience fueled with adrenaline, water bottles, and six months of anticipation.

When the gun finally went off hurtling us into the twenty-six-mile trek, I was experiencing such a high that I barely noticed the rain that had begun to fall. With all the hoopla and excitement, one thing that slipped my attention was the blister that began to form on the sole of my now water-soaked foot. Four miles later, in Brooklyn, Mr. Blister introduced itself to me with a searing, burning pain. A blister may not sound like a big deal to you, but when you're in pain on the fourth mile of a twenty-six-mile race, a blister can make for a very long day.

After all the months of preparation, I decided to steel myself and not pay attention to the burning that accompanied the squish, squishing of my shoes.

Midway into the race, climbing the gentle slope up the Pulaski Bridge in Queens, I found that I had more to worry about than my burning foot. Everything just seemed to come unraveled. In spite of my training and better sense, I had given in to adrenaline and wound up running much faster than planned. I was beginning to feel a deep fatigue and tightness in my legs. But this was only thirteen miles into the race! And whether I walked or ran, I still had thirteen miles to go before reaching Central Park. A kind of depression set in, a hopeless and trapped feeling. After six months of training, planning, and sacrifice, this just couldn't be happening. But it was. Putting it bluntly, all I wanted to do was quit.

I would have quit running, this I'm sure. But at exactly that moment I noticed a banner draped over the side of an apartment house. The banner must have been two stories high. It showed the now-famous Nike swoosh logo, along with the caption *Just Do It!* I don't know if Nike had introduced this banner for the race, but it was the first time I had seen it. Through the haze of negativity I read those words and remember smiling. Something in me shifted. In my semiconscious brooding, those words took root—Just do it! I found someone inside me talking: *Yes, that's it! Stop whining. Come on, Joe, just do it!* It made perfect sense. In that moment I was able to totally and completely believe the simplicity of the revelation that had come to me. It was like magic, cutting through and shredding my doubts as if they were merely idle childish thoughts that had to be dismissed. Every time my focus would come back to the squishing of aching feet or the burning of muscles in my legs, I would reprimand myself and once again insist, *Just do it!*

I finished the race in a respectable four hours. In spite of my postrace discomfort, I was elated. Considering how I felt at thirteen miles, it was nothing short of amazing that I had managed to finish at all. How did this happen? It wasn't my thinking the phrase *Just do it!* that enabled me to turn defeat into success that day, it was my willingness to *believe*

215

the simplicity of Nike's formula. When you combine positive thinking with complete conviction, the outcome will often seem quite miraculous. The motivational formula that I would like to offer you is this:

50% positive thinking + 50% positively believing = success

Self-doubt, negativity, and insecurity can form a sturdy tripod that resists being toppled. To succeed, you're going to have to challenge the thoughts that support each leg of this tripod and then risk believing the truth. Motivation to me is synonymous with believing (or a willingness to risk believing) that you can do what you set out to do or handle what life challenges you with. When you harness the attitude that insists you're going to risk believing that you can—you will! The belief that sustains you over time and continues to motivate you results from four facts:

1. *Pain.* Your struggle is painful. Your life reflects the contamination of insecurity and control, and you're fed up. You want more, and you deserve it. You're damn tired of battling. *This is motivating.*

2. *Awareness.* You must develop adequate awareness of what's really going on in your life. You need to know what to change, and how to change, and you need to be convinced that you can do it. It all breaks down to those two important words I told you about early in this book: control and habit. Knowing what's happening can empower you with the knowledge that all habits are learned, and all habits can be broken. *This is motivating.*

3. *Success.* The more success you have, the more you will develop confidence and momentum. This energy will encourage you to embrace the right attitude: a willingness to risk believing that you can let go of control. *This is motivating.*

4. *Happiness.* As you risk letting go of control and risk believing in yourself, you will begin to experience happiness. Once you taste true happiness, you'll never trade it in for the narrow-minded, controlling, insecure life of struggle you've known. *This is motivating.*

Protecting Your Motivation

When you begin working on your motivation, it's important to realize that insecurity is never going to simply roll over and die; it's always going to be looking for your Achilles' heel—your weak spots. Early in your efforts, you need to be on guard to protect yourself from needless sabotage. Look at the following list of typical sabotaging, motivation-dampening responses and study the proactive, coached responses that will get you through these challenges:

Sabotaging Thinking	Proactive Coaching
Yes, but . . .	No, not *yes, but. Yes,* period! There's no *but* about it. *But* is another word for self-doubt. I don't have to allow every positive thought to be drowned out by my insecurity. From now on I'm going to risk just saying *yes.*
If only . . .	When did I ever become so powerless? Instead of hoping to be more effective, I'm going to choose to be! Hoping is hesitating. No more hesitation for me!
I can't . . .	There's a showstopper right there! Who says *I can't*? No more Reflexive Thinking for me. It only feels like *I can't.* The truth is, I can, I will, I must!
I should . . .	No more compulsion for me. Who's been running my life, anyway? It's time I start figuring out what I *want* to do rather than what I *should* do.
I have to . . .	Who says? I can choose strength and decide to call all the shots. From now on it's not whether I *have* to, it's whether I *want* to!
What if . . .	There I go, always projecting those negatives. If I decide I can handle what life

	throws at me, I don't have to be worrying about what-ifs.
I'm not smart enough (good-looking enough, etc.) . . .	Another excuse! Time to admit the truth and stop hiding behind lame fears. The only way I'll ever know is to try.
It's too hard . . .	Poor baby! So what if it's hard? I'm harder! I can do whatever I set my mind to do. I'm tired of giving up before I try.
Nothing ever turns out right for me.	From now on it's not what's behind me that matters, it's what's in front of me. No more thinking like a failure for me!

Motivation: The Coaching Part

Self-Coaching insists that you already possess everything you need. Because of self-doubt, distrust, and insecurity, you've become estranged from your true source of power. The only way to reclaim your power is to take it. Think about it. If you know you can win, if you have a plan, and if you know it's doable, why not go for it? A good coach will take a despondent team and lay out a manageable plan of attack, one that pits reason and objectivity against the blockage created by doubt. Once this plan is laid out, it's up to the coach to ignite a fire of enthusiasm— to motivate the team and energize momentum.

You are both coach and athlete. The spark you bring is the grounded belief in one simple fact: you can change your life. You really can! This is your spark. Now that you've got your five-step plan for creating the life you want, the only thing left is to let yourself feel the desire—that taste-in-your-mouth feeling of success. And once you feel the desire, then ask one more question: "What's stopping me?" The answer: nothing! There's nothing in your way. There never was!

Self-Coaching Reflection
Motivation isn't mysterious.
It's the energy you feel when you're willing
to risk believing that you can change your life.

PART IV

Living with the Power of Self-Coaching

16

Use Your Power

Now is the time I step back and allow you to experience the power and strength of your own Self-Coaching. Now that you're ready to implement what you've learned, I don't feel I need to make any pledges or promises—the proof, as they say, is in the pudding. And what more proof will you need than to realize that you're ready and able to take your life back from insecurity's grasp?

I can't guarantee you success or happiness in life, but you can! With a Self-Coached attitude, you can demand it! Do keep in mind that when Reflexive Thinking has been your habit for a long time, change may feel unnatural at first. Fortunately, this feeling is only temporary. Once you taste a life of spontaneity and trust, you won't be looking back over your shoulder. One thing about living life on the happy side of the fence: it's exhilarating. Be patient, be strong, and stick to the program. The quality of your life depends on it!

Putting It All Together

*I wanted to change the world. But I have found that the only thing
one can be sure of changing is oneself.*

—Aldous Huxley

Imagine growing up in a protected courtyard enclosed on all sides by twenty-foot-high stone walls. Let us also imagine that from birth, you never ventured beyond your four walls. Your only perceptions would be your walls; the sky above; the rhythmic transits of the sun, moon and stars; occasionally some rain or snow; visitations from a few curious local birds; and an occasional leaf carried by the wind. If I asked you what you thought about life, you might shrug your shoulders and insist that the world is an altogether dull place without much opportunity. You might go on to report that you feel quite safe and secure, but lament the lack of passion or interest in your life. You wouldn't forget to tell me of your interminable boredom, which at times seems almost unbearable. But mostly, I suspect, you'd be anguishing over the loneliness and lack of intimacy in your life.

In a stone-walled courtyard, none of your above reporting would be false; it would be a reality dictated by the circumstances of your enclosure. It wouldn't be fair to say that your reality is distorted. It's just limited. This limited, courtyard view is exactly what control does to your life. It narrows your field of view and leaves you convinced that the world is a place with few choices, a place where you're a prisoner—confined and helpless. I hope that by this point in your reading you've come to understand that there is a whole world of choice just beyond your courtyard of Reflexive Thinking. I'm certain of one thing: once you leave your prison of controlled living, you'll never return.

Habit and Control: The Keys to Change

Change requires action, not reflection; motivation, not passivity; desire, not apathy; and a willingness to see truth rather than fiction. But most important, change requires that you recognize that no one and nothing is going to change you—except you. Wrestle with this concept if you must, but unless you're ready to take full responsibility for changing your life, don't expect too much.

One thing I set out to accomplish at the outset of this book was to make sure that if nothing else, I was able to convince you that a struggling, unhappy life results from the constrictive habits you've accumulated trying too hard to control life. Habit and control. Understand these two concepts and I assure you that no problem big or small will ever confuse you again. Let's complete our review of these two vital-concepts.

Habit

If we eliminate circumstantial problems (problems *not* driven by inse-curity but by reality, such as job loss, illness, or a tax audit), then the rest of your problems, whether they be anger, stress, unhappiness, inef-fectiveness, loneliness, anxiety, phobia, panic, or depression, need to be seen for what they are: habits that *are* driven by insecurity. *Habits.* Say this word again and again. And now take it one step further: all habits are learned, and any habit can be broken!

One of the first things I do when someone comes to me for therapy is to neutralize the effects of insecurity. Take panic, for example. When someone begins to tell me how out of control or crazy he or she feels, or that he or she can't handle life, I respond in a casual and unruffled manner, in stark contrast to that person's intensity, "I can see how all this frightens you, but do you realize that anxiety is *just* a habit?" From the very start, my job is to counter the destructive, at times hysterical, energy connected to these habits of insecurity. (How about you? Since you've been working with your five steps, have you noticed that you're less inclined to exaggerate your problems?)

Again and again I need to deflate the exaggerated, insecurity-driven feelings that life can't be handled. Don, a burly construction worker in his midtwenties, was having a difficult time with anxiety, sleeping, and constant worry. He became a bit unsettled during our first session when I didn't seem to share his urgency: "But, Doctor, I don't think you understand. I feel like I'm losing my mind. I can't take much more of this!" To this I responded with seasoned calmness: "It's your habit of anxiety that has you confused and convinced that you can't handle life. Just because you feel this way doesn't mean it's true. Habits can easily distort how you see things. When someone quits smoking, and that person feels that he or she can't live without another cigarette, do you think this is true? Do you think that person will die? Or do you think it's the nicotine habit talking? Just like the guy quitting smoking, you need to figure out who's telling you that you can't handle life: is it you, or is it your habit of insecurity?"

Whenever someone tries to convince me that insecurity-driven problems are real, my first response is to throw water on the fire with the altogether insubordinate attitude of *no big deal!* I pay very little attention to the apocalyptic concerns or fears, and instead treat all Reflexive Thinking with an attitude of dismissal: *it's just your habit.* Although most people struggle at first with my seemingly indifferent attitude (because it seems counterintuitive to what they've been feeling), when it finally registers in their own mind that their psychological struggles are just habits, the effect can be startling. It's the moment when they recognize, "Hey, maybe I really can change. I can handle habits!"

I'd like you to begin to incorporate this attitude from now on. Get used to challenging your frantic, negative, or defeatist thinking with an understated attitude of calm: "In spite of how I feel, I know it's *just* a habit."

I sometimes take another approach when someone tells me life is too hard or they'll never be happy. I go for a more dramatic effect, trying to get them to learn to laugh at the ridiculousness of these fantasies. If you're being driven by primitive, absurd habits of insecurity, try hard to laugh (out loud helps) at how preposterous it is that you to go on believing this nonsense.

When you can take a lighter, less serious view of your Reflexive Thinking, you'll be in a good position to notice the very primitive, childlike quality of these lamentations. Once you look, you'll find it hard to miss the whiny, whimpering, and altogether exaggerated quality of these responses. Most people pay far too much attention to this drivel that insecurity throws at them. If you decide to lose weight, do you think it helps to whine about how miserable you feel? Or if you happen to be a worrywart, can you tell me what good it does to worry about whether you'll ever have a heart attack? Or get fired? Or find a soul mate? Don't start moaning that you can't find a job, or a husband, or that nothing ever works out for you. Instead ask yourself, *Why am I listening to insecurity?* If you're honest, you can only conclude that there is no reason—no truthful, objective reason—just your habit of insecurity distorting the facts.

I don't care how you accomplish it—laughing at how ridiculous you sound, realizing how child-connected your habit is, or recognizing the simple truth that habits can be broken; whatever it takes, just *stop paying attention* by Changing the Channel, becoming a tad more reckless, or using what you've learned in your meditation practice.

Four Ways to Beat Any Habit

1. Begin to cultivate a lighter, less serious response to your struggle. Take the air out of these problems by minimizing rather than maximizing their importance. Anxiety—just a habit! Depression—just a habit! Lack of success—just a habit! Unhappiness—just a habit!

2. Notice the primitive, child connection to your Reflexive Thinking. Tell yourself, *If I were to say this thought out loud, people would laugh at me.* Admit how silly you sound when you whine and moan about not being able to handle life.

3. Inject consciousness into the picture using Self-Talk. It's time to replace fiction with fact. You now realize why you don't need to control life. Be courageous enough to simply live it!

4. Fortified with your new perspective, go out and win a few battles. Start with a few small challenges and build some momentum and confidence.

❖ ❖ ❖

SELF-COACHING POWER DRILL

Listen carefully to other adults for the next day or two. (At first you might find it easier to notice this childlike quality when it comes from someone else.) See how many times you hear a perfectly normal adult act like a panicky, weak, or fragile child: "I can't take this, it's too hard. I'm just not strong enough to handle it." Or, "Oh, my God, what if he doesn't talk to me? What will I do? My life will be ruined." Or, "I'm so depressed. Just leave me alone. I need to be alone." Recognizing the child connection will also give you a glimpse into the origins of these habits. Listen to yourself when insecurity steers your thoughts. It's like getting a ride in a time machine—right back to your childhood, where these habits were forged.

Seeing your problems for exactly what they are—bad habits—will change your whole perspective. I hope by now you're growing weary of my refrain, *habits are learned, and habits can be broken.* You've seen it in your life and in the lives of others. Habits are patterns of behavior and thinking that have become reflexive. Because habits become automatic, you need to inject some consciousness in the form of Self-Talk into the picture. It will seem unnatural at first, but that's only because you're used to reflexive living, not because it *is* natural.

Out, Damn Tick

Sometimes it helps to work with metaphors. Imagine that habits are like parasites, with you being the host. A habit (if we ascribe a form of consciousness to it) doesn't want to be extinguished; it wants to live— at your expense, of course! Your habit wants you, but more important, it *needs* you if it's going to survive. And to succeed, your habit must control how you think. It does this through Reflexive Thinking. Once Reflexive Thinking takes over, your habit has it made. Your vital life energy is being sucked out of you as your habit grows stronger and stronger.

This is the reason why people will say: "I don't understand, I was fine until last month. I never had an anxiety attack before. Now, out of nowhere, I'm a basket case. How can this happen all of a sudden?" But it didn't happen all of a sudden. Your habit took time to grow and flourish; then, when it reached critical mass—*wham!* At this point your habit owns you. More than likely, your habit had been under construction for years, and only when you reached the tipping point did you become aware that the symptoms of your life had gone awry.

My dog Lulu had something on her neck last week. At first I

thought it was a growth; it was a gray-blue cylinder about half an inch long—gross. After putting on my reading glasses for a closer look, I happened to notice a few small black legs protruding at the growth's base—ah-ha. This was no growth, this was a tick! After yanking out the gruesome critter, I was quite impressed with the tick's tenacity and unwillingness to release my Lulu. A tick is a parasite. Habits are like parasites—tenacious and unwilling to yield. Stop feeding your parasites!

No doubt about it: habits, like ticks, are stubborn. They require some work and effort to snap them loose. Remember, it's *just your habit* of insecurity that stands between you and the changed life you want. Nothing else.

Control: Keep It Simple

Back in the fourteenth century, a philosopher and Franciscan friar, William of Occam, is said to have advanced the principle of parsimony, which states, "Of two competing theories or explanations, all other things being equal, the simpler one is to be preferred." According to Occam's razor (which it is now popularly called), if last night a violent storm blew through your neighborhood and in the morning you noticed a shingle from your roof lying on the ground, the simplest solution would be that the wind blew it off. This explanation requires one assumption. If, however, you wanted to assert that some extraterrestrial visitor was trying to infiltrate your house, this explanation would require quite a few assumptions (the first of which would be to accept the existence of aliens) to eventually reach the same conclusion.

When it comes to a shingle on the ground, it seems like a no-brainer—of course it was the wind. Well, to me the law of parsimony holds true for psychology. The simple solution is to understand that control is at the center of all your problems—no need for any theoretical debate here. So if you have problems, if your life has stagnated, if you struggle, all you need to do is ask yourself one simple and important question: *What am I trying to control?* When, for example, you find yourself worrying about what your boyfriend's going to say, ask, "What am I trying to control?" When you're trying too hard to look good at the office because you feel you're a loser, ask, "What am I trying to control?" Or when you're trying to avoid your neighbor because you think he's mad at you, once again ask, "What am I trying to control?"

A situation where you find yourself fretting *I can't handle this* becomes fertile ground for doubt and distrust, and from this soil Reflexive Thinking flourishes. But please be clear on this point. It may appear that control is the antidote to chaos: "If I can just make them like me, then I'll have nothing to worry about." The truth is, a controlling life eventually guarantees chaos. Maybe not today or tomorrow, but eventually it will wear you down and turn your life upside down. I hope that by now I've been able to convince you that controlling life is an illusion. It's never a feasible goal, and eventually the pursuit becomes the problem.

Now you know what you've got to do, so when it comes to conflict, get used to asking, "How is this related to control?" If you don't ask, if you're not looking for the simple answer, then you're apt to be misled: "It's my anxiety that prevents me from making that call." Nope, it's not your anxiety, or your depression, or the way your mother punished you when you were a child—stop looking to complicate the picture. The simple truth is you're struggling because you're trying to control life. And trying so hard to control life is why you're getting anxious in the first place.

If you've been captured by control's seductive promises, you're headed for big trouble. As one bumper sticker I saw said, *Where am I going and why am I in this handbasket?* Once your life is handed over to control, there can be no choice, only compulsion, fear, and doubt—it's straight to hell in the old handbasket.

Struggling That Lasts Too Long

Everyone occasionally encounters difficult, chronic problems that can leave one feeling victimized and hopeless. Whether it is a long-standing lack of success in love or career, a chronic illness, or just general unhappiness, whenever you get caught up in a struggle that won't quit, there's a tendency to lose perspective and hope. I was doing a TV call-in show a while ago, discussing the anxieties of our troubled times, and heard this from a distraught caller:

My wife is in the army and has been shipped to Iraq, leaving me here with our two young children. I always knew it was difficult managing two toddlers, but I had no idea just how difficult it was. I'm not sure I can handle this. I work during the day, pick up the kids at day care, come home, and it's feed, play, and bathe. I don't stop for one minute. I never had this much responsibility. I'm worried sick about my wife, but I'm really scared about handling this situation. The kids are always crying and asking when Mommy's coming home. I don't know what to tell them anymore. I want to scream. I can't do this. I'm just not strong enough. What can I do?

Obviously this caller was overwhelmed and panicky. Part of the problem when dealing with a stressful, prolonged crisis is that we begin to deplete ourselves physically as well as emotionally. When this happens, your normal resilience is lowered and you begin to feel as if you're unraveling (losing control). In a situation like this, it's imperative to stop any further depletion. I tried to help the caller recognize that his number-one priority was to try to restore his own resilience. And short of his wife walking in the door, he was going to need to do this by regaining a sense of perspective.

The caller needed to stop seeing everything simultaneously. We have a tendency when in crisis mode to allow our fears, worries, anticipations, and doubts to blind us all at once. What's called for in situations like this is a methodical and disciplined approach to regaining some balance. I suggested that the caller begin focusing on each here-and-now task, one at a time, without thinking about how he was going to manage tomorrow's challenges. If he was feeding the kids, I wanted him to just be feeding the kids and not thinking about how he was going to manage getting them ready for bed.

By staying focused on one manageable task at a time, you don't allow thoughts to wander into the what-if mode of Reflexive Thinking. Sure, it takes a leap of faith to tell yourself, "I'm going to figure it all out—one challenge at a time," but as I told the caller, it's a risk that makes all the difference. Becoming task-oriented rather than having a head full of what-ifs can quickly make life more manageable. But then comes the real challenge: cultivating trust. Trust to risk believing that come tomorrow, you'll handle things! The moment you accept the belief that you'll handle it is the moment the anxiety goes away.

Sometimes, as with an acute crisis—such as your boss finding out that you were complaining about him—it's just a matter of getting beyond the shock wave of adversity. But with ongoing, chronic challenges you will need to develop a more disciplined mind-set. This more adaptive mind-set begins with the objective realization that human beings have an instinctive ability to survive. When we're not confused by Reflexive Thinking, we naturally find ways of coping with any challenging situation.

Think about it: Do you remember yesterday's problems? Last month's? Last year's? What happened to all those problems? Where are they now? They're like a fist: once you open your hand, they vanish. You've managed to handle countless obstacles and challenges in your life, and you've gotten through each and every one—somehow. And guess what? You haven't quit yet (if you had, you wouldn't be reading this book). Insecurity can make you forget about the thousands of problems you've handled in the past and instead leave you saying, "But this time is different. I don't know if I can handle this one."

From this point on, no more fortune-telling. Like my advice to the caller to the TV show, start with a task orientation. Next, using Self-Talk, learn to stop the train of Reflexive Thoughts that constantly remind you about what's missing in your life. Instead, replace the negatives with an objective assessment of the opportunities that do exist. And please don't say you have no opportunities or options.

Julie, a single woman I was working with, had just turned forty. She felt there were options—all negative:

> I'm forty and single. I'm getting some gray hairs, I'm beginning to notice some sagging here and there, my hair is different—less manageable. I'm over the hill and it's all going to get worse. I've

been unhappy for a long time, but now I've got something to really be upset about. There's nothing you can say to make it any different. I'm forty and I'm going to wake up being forty tomorrow! Life has passed me by, and what's ahead looks very dark.

I asked Julie to reflect a moment and imagine that she were fifty years old. Then I asked her to tell me, at fifty, how she would feel being forty again. Julie responded:

Well, let's see. If I were fifty, I guess one of the first things I'd say would be, "I'd give anything to be forty again." Actually, it's funny you should ask me this, because it's exactly what I said to myself the other day, "I'd give anything to be thirty." And you know, I probably was doing the same thing when I was thirty. Okay, so what you're telling me is that someday I'll see my present situation differently, less negatively. And I know that's true, but it doesn't make me feel any better.

It didn't make Julie feel any better because she was being petulant—she still wanted to see what was wrong with her life. This was part of her controlling juggle—clinging desperately to her youth in a vain, frightened, unrealistic attempt to control life. As primitive as it may sound (and as you know, control can be pretty primitive), she wanted magically not to grow older. Fortunately, this resistance—and childishness—didn't last long. She began to see the bigger picture. The bigger picture was that being forty years old wasn't her problem, it was her insecurity-driven perception of what being forty meant—the end of the world! Julie began living her days with more gusto, looking ahead with courage rather than fear and negative projections. No more fortune-telling for Julie.

I bet you know what I'm going to say next. It's been five years since I saw Julie. I just received a picture of her and her new husband, standing in front of the Eiffel Tower. Julie's smile made me smile. I couldn't help thinking, *I told you so!*

Self-Coaching Reflection
The past cannot dictate your future unless you let it.

Tombstone Lessons

Life is change and life is choice. As long as you don't get bottled up in a limited, courtyard mentality, you'll be fine. I remember when this notion that *life is choice* first lit up my life. I was in graduate school and was involved in my PIG (personal identity and growth) group. We were talking about death and dying and other such control fears when our group leader asked a rather poignant question: what we would want written on our tombstones. As unsettling as this notion was, it appealed to me.

I did a little research and found, for example, that Edgar Allan Poe's gravestone reads, *Quoth the Raven, "Nevermore."* And Will Rogers's epitaph states, *I never met a man I didn't like.* How would I sum up my life? After a few days or so it came to me quite unexpectedly. I decided that I wanted my epitaph to read, *I'd rather be reading this.*

"I'd rather be reading this" is my way of telling the world that my preference is life. And life is choice. Only death is choiceless. Once in a while, when life pelts me with too many obstacles, I remember that I'm alive, and as long as I'm alive, I'll be okay. And if I'm not feeling okay, then I'll do whatever it takes to change! Of course, there are always those who will moan, saying they're trying to change, but they just can't be happy until they get into that particular college, land that job, or marry Mr. Right. If your happiness depends on what's on the other side of the mountain, then for your sake, I hope you have good climbing shoes.

Spontaneous living requires living with trust. Sure, it's a risk to let go of the false gods of control and just live life instead of trying to anticipate and prepare for it. Some will feel this is a reckless way to live, but that's only because they have so little trust in their ability to respond to life from a source other than Reflexive Thinking. But once you step out of control's box and realize a whole new world of effort-less, unrehearsed living, you'll understand why no one ever returns to their courtyard, why no one ever longs for the old days of control and rigidity.

Before I leave the altogether morbid topic of tombstones, I want to mention an e-mail that was recently forwarded to me. It was about a man who, during a eulogy, pointed out that although the dates of birth and death are recorded on a tombstone, they're not important. What's really important is the *dash* between the two dates—because that dash represents an entire life that has taken place. As long as you are in your dash years, nothing is written in stone (pun intended). With Self-Coaching you can create whatever kind of dash suites you. After all, it's your dash.

Serenity Now

Self-Coaching may not be able to change all the circumstances of your life, but it can change your experience of life. In spite of any fantasies you may harbor, no matter how hard you look, you're not going to find a life without problems. Life is a challenge for everyone, not just you. Just as there are rainy days and sunny days, health and sickness, life is what it is: a challenge. And an opportunity. If you insist that life "should" be different (as opposed to you becoming different), then you're still caught up in chasing control's rainbow of illusion.

Control will try to whisper in your ear that you can avoid difficulty—if only you try a bit harder to become more perfect, to worry a just a wee bit longer, or perhaps to become slightly craftier. Yes, control can be subtle, seductive, compelling, even hypnotic, but you know my preferred view: control is a parasite that sucks your vital energy! To find happiness and meaning in your life, you need to find balance. With balance comes serenity.

The purpose of Self-Coaching is to restore self-confidence and trust, a willingness to believe that you can handle what life throws at you. Handling life, all of life, this is the ultimate achievement. Control's selling point is to convince you that you can somehow, if you just try hard enough, avoid what threatens you. By now you should know better. You really can deal with adversity, and as long as you have trust, you don't have to know how or what you'll do. If you do happen to fall, you'll know in your heart that all you have to do is dust yourself off and stand once again.

Once you recognize that you don't need to avoid, deflect, or otherwise sidestep life, you are in a position to understand the concept of balance. Whether it is paying your bills, cleaning your house, or standing up to a bully, a balanced life is one where you willingly accept responsibility. Accepting responsibility is synonymous with accepting life. Only children—and adults who act like children—are shielded from responsibility. The mature pursuit is to accept your life, the good and the bad, and to deal with it directly.

You've probably heard Reinhold Niebuhr's Serenity Prayer:

God, give us grace to accept with serenity the things that cannot be changed, courage to change the things which should be changed, and the wisdom to distinguish the one from the other.

Let's look at the prayer's first challenge: *to accept with serenity the things that cannot be changed.* In everyone's life there are obstacles. These can be physical or psychological limitations, external demands and responsibilities, or other unique circumstances. All too often, when faced with significant adversity, we become mired in self-pity and feelings of victimization. Ruth, a young woman in her early twenties whom I met a few years ago, was the tragic victim of a drunken driver. She suffered irreversible spinal damage and is confined to a wheelchair. She told me that her worst enemy isn't her disability, it's her self-pity. Another word for self-pity is nonacceptance. To accept those things that cannot be changed—with serenity—is a supreme goal, for only then are you free to move forward with your life.

The second challenge is for *the courage to change the things which should be changed.* Throughout this book I've mentioned the need to risk trusting. The precursor to risking is courage. Courage is strength of will to believe that we can withstand and handle danger, fear, or difficulty. Standing up against control can be a truly frightening experience, but with a foundation of understanding and truth, you should be able to muster up the necessary courage. And don't ever forget that courage is a choice.

Also notice the word *should* in this sentence: things which *should* be changed. This is one of the rare times I will allow you to say *should*. There is a normal, healthy, happy, and spontaneous you that depends on living life to its fullest. And you *should* demand this. To go a step further, you *must* demand this! Change whatever needs to be changed to achieve the life you were meant to live.

The final challenge is to have *the wisdom to distinguish the one from the other.* Control distorts as well as limits your perception of life. The wisdom to distinguish truth from fiction has been a constant refrain throughout this book. Ask yourself, when you first picked up this book, what were your truths? Did you harbor doubts about yourself? Did you feel that your life was never going to be satisfying? Did you feel that you could never change? These are distortions I hope you're ready to dispel. At least now you have the tools to dismantle Reflexive Thinking and begin distinguishing the one (fact) from the other (fiction).

Self-Coaching Reflection
Take responsibility for your thoughts:
because they become actions.
Take responsibility for your actions:
because they become habits.
Take responsibility for your habits:
because they become your personality.
Take responsibility for your personality:
because it will become your destiny.

The key to creating the life you want is your willingness to accept *responsibility* for it. Responsibility for your thoughts, for what you tell yourself, and most important, for what you listen to. Do this, and everything else will follow. At some point you will decide whether it's time to take responsibility for your life. Is that time now? Have you struggled enough? Only you can decide.

Index

Index

Printed in the United States of America

ED-12-18-10